War Bike:
British Military Motorcycling 1899-1919

War Bike:
British Military Motorcycling 1899-1919
Martin Gegg

Centenary Edition
Published by Fenland Classic Motorcycles
www.Fenlandclassics.com

1918-2018

Copyright © 2018 Martin Gegg

The right of Martin Gegg to be identified as the Author of the work has been asserted by him in accordance with the Copyright, Designs and Patents Act 1988

All rights reserved. This book or any portion thereof may not be reproduced or used in any manner whatsoever without the express written permission of the publisher in writing, except for the use of brief quotations in a book review or scholarly journal.

First Published: September 2015

Centenary Edition January 2018

ISBN 978-1-326-40667-7

Dedication

© Crown copyright 2014

At the time of writing this, we are approaching the 100th anniversary of the start of the First World War.

I was privileged to witness first-hand the Remembrance Service in Whitehall on 11 November 2008 attended by the last three surviving allied soldiers involved in the War. They have now all passed away and it is important that we commemorate the memory of all those across the world affected by the War. In particular the sacrifice each man woman and child endured, both during the War itself, and following the armistice in November 1918.

The statistics are staggering; the War, together with the Spanish flu pandemic that followed, had a profound effect on economic development in the early 20th Century. 940,658[1] allied[2] armed forces personnel were killed or later died as a result of their injuries[3] and a further 2,095,347 allied soldiers were injured[4] It is estimated a total of 37 million people were killed or wounded and countless others across the Globe lost their homes or had their lives radically altered as a result of this conflict.

This book is dedicated to the memory of every person involved.

---

[1] Statistics of the Military Effort of the British Empire, British Library Ref: 9085.h.13.
[2] Includes Commonwealth and Colonies Excludes USA (116,708)
[3] Since been revised to 1,116,371 by the Commonwealth War Graves Commission based on graves and those commemorated on Memorials.
[4] Statistics of the Military Effort of the British Empire, British Library Ref: 9085.h.13.

Contents

Acknowledgements ix
Introduction 1
1: Early Experimentation 3
2: Birth of the Despatch Rider 7
3: War Office Procurement 15
4: The Clouds Gather 23
5: Mobilisation August 1914 27
6: Life on the Front Line 33
7: The Military Motorcycle in 1914 39
8: Customisation & Standardisation 43
9: The War Years 47
    1915 Developments 47
    1916 Developments 50
    1917 Developments 53
    1918 Developments 58
    1919 Developments 61
10: The Intelligence Corps 63
11: Competitions & Record Breaking 65
12: Sidecars, Gun Carriers & Ambulances 71
    Sidecars 71
    Gun Carriers 72
    Ambulances 80
13: Women Motorcyclists at War 83
14: Pigeon Carriers 87
15: Recycling and Repair 89
16: Motorcycle Numbers & Manufacturers 93
17: Postscript 101

Contents Cont....

Bibliography 102

Glossary 103

Acknowledgements

The 'spark' for this book started with a few notes about testing Military Motorcycles at Brooklands and expanded into an extensive research project. I would like to thank the Brooklands Motorcycle Volunteer Team for inspiring me to write this book.

Special thanks go to the Brooklands Museum Curatorial and Library Staff who gave invaluable assistance in gathering material and research support. The Museum Library has a vast archive of track records concerning Riders/Drivers, Cars and Motorcycles, as well as a comprehensive library of Brooklands related history books. I was privileged to gain access to the photographic archive which contains some stunning images.

In particular, I would like to thank Roger Bird with his encyclopedic knowledge of Brooklands and expertise in Pioneer Motorcycling; and to Steve Madill, for valuable images and in particular helping to identify Frank Houghton, who organised the 1915 Brooklands Services Events.

Thanks in no particular order also to:

- James Hewing and the National Motorcycle Museum for access to their Clyno Motor Machine Gun Carrier which helped me understand the engineering behind these machines.

- Gareth Mears, the Archivist at the Royal Logistics Corps Museum who provided the Annual Reports of The Mechanical Transport Committee. These records gave a fascinating insight into the procurement process.

- James Robinson of The Classic Motorcycle and Mortons Media for contemporary images.

- Ivor Ramsden of The Manx Aviation & Military Museum for images of Despatch Riders and Phelon & Moore motorcycles.

- John Watson who has provided me with the story behind the first military sidecar body for Phelon and Moore.

- David Venner for excerpts from the diary of Albert Simkin MM.

- My editor wife who has been an invaluable source of support and encouragement.

On-line sources: I am indebted to the many people who shared information and images through the Great War Forum.

Writing this reference book has been an interesting journey, and I hope goes some small way to dispel myths attached to this era, The contents are a tribute to all of the people who played vital roles up to and during WW1: whether in the Field, on the Home Front or quietly on the domestic Front: All Served and All are Remembered.

Photographs

Front Cover:

Despatch Rider Stanley Caroll (Manx Aviation & Military Museum)

The Author has individually acknowledged Copyright holders. Some of the images were published in contemporary reports and maybe out of Copyright. Please contact the author if any entry generates copyright issues.

Email: Warbike@Fenlandclassics.co.uk

Introduction

The First World War is generally regarded as the 'first' mechanised conflict. At the outbreak of war motor vehicles and aircraft were still at developmental stage; then understandably, transportation of troops and the delivery of weapons underwent a 'quantum leap' at this time of conflict.

The introduction of a revolutionary Land Ship "The Tank" capable of delivering shells from a highly mobile protective platform; and aircraft, which at the start of the conflict were used for artillery spotting, set the scene for fully fledged fighting and bombing machines.

And even though less direct evidence exists to suggest motorcycles underwent the same level of *conflict-generated* technical development, they did play a significant part on every Front and in every major conflict since.

This book tells the story of how after a slow start the humble motor-bicycle became accepted as an essential part of battlefield logistics and communication.

1: Early Experimentation

In the late 1800's, when Bicycle manufacturers and engineers first experimented with small engines in bicycle frames, the motorcycle was born and *revved* its way into automotive history. Military authorities did not pursue the idea of motorcycling for warfare use, but an enthusiastic entrepreneur and pioneer of the British Motor Industry, Frederick Simms realised military backing had potential to drive future development, and deliver significant financial reward.

The earliest example of such a vehicle was the Simms Motor-Scout; a Maxim gun mounted on a Beeston Quadricycle powered by a de-Dion Bouton engine was demonstrated by Frederick Simms at the Richmond Automobile Show in June 1899.

Simms Demonstrating The Motor Scout in 1899   (Mortons)

The following November, just one month after the beginning of the Second Boer War, Edwin Emerson in the American Automobile

War Bike: British Military Motorcycling 1899-1919

Magazine imagines Simms's Motor Scout in action as part of a mobile force of Armoured Cars and quick-firing Automobile Batteries,[5] yet still there is no evidence the War Office placed an order. This prototype was claimed in 1914 to be the earliest example of an armoured gun-mounted motor-cycle[6].

The Motor Scout in Action (The Automobile Magazine Nov 1899)

---

[5] Emerson E, The Automobile Magazine, November 1899, P116
[6] The Motor Cycle, 1 October 1914, P391

Whilst the Motor Scout may represent the earliest gun mounted motor-cycle, the 26th Middlesex Cyclist Volunteer Reserve had already used a motorised Tri-cycle to tow a Maxim gun during Easter manoeuvres in Aldershot. The tri-cycle, developed by Mr Charter of the Cyclometer Company and Sergeant "Jack" Rule of the Cycle Battalion[7] appears to be a further development of the various pedal bicycle combinations that were in use to transport Maxim Guns at this time.

Motorised Tricycle Easter 1899 (Army & Navy Illustrated 22 April 1899)

By 1900 about 50 manufacturers of motorised Tri-cycles were in existence; they were relatively common and far more robust than their two wheel counterpart. The Motor Manufacturing Company was awarded a contract to supply the War Office with a number of 2¼ hp Tri-cycles for use in the Boer War[8]. As yet the author has found no evidence of their use in Action.

---

[7] Parker-Galbreath S, The Birth of the London Cycle Corps & 26th Middlesex Battalion, http://www.25thlondon.com/26thhistory.htm
[8] Walford EW, Early Days in the British Motorcycle Industry P32.

During the Second Boar War, cycles were widely used in the field. There were experiments using cycles for delivering dispatches, but still regarded as unsatisfactory at the time, when horsepower remained the fastest way to travel. In June 1901, towards the end of the Boer War, M.P. for the New Forest, John Scot Montague (later Lord Montague of Beaulieu) urged the Government to follow the lead of France and Germany, and consider motorcycles for military use[9].

The British Regular Army of the early 1900s was a highly mobile force, still reliant on Cavalry and Infantry, with logistical support provided by Horses and Mules; and perhaps a common misconception exists that the Army had no interest in replacing the horse. This view persisted in some quarters until after the end of the First World War, but the reality was that the Army remained keen to explore efficiencies in the supply train, whilst keeping the Cavalry in a primary role.

Experiments followed with mechanical transport by steam powered traction engines during the Boer War, and as mechanical transport developed, extended their experimentation to include motorised transport; resulting In the Mechanical Transport Committee responsible for experimentation and reporting in 1900.

This time (early 1900's) represents a major period of change for the British Army: complex planning and strategies for the defence of the British Empire would need updating if wagon trains of the past were to be replaced by railways and motorised transport.

In the next two chapters we deal with campaigning for use of motorcycles, and their role in the Army's mechanical transport system.

---

[9] Hansard: HC Deb, 06 June 1901, Vol 94 column 1261.

2: Birth of the Despatch Rider

In the years following the Boer War the pedal Cycle Despatch Corps became the primary means of delivering dispatches. Towards the end of the decade motorcycles had advanced further and there were suggestions for the use of motorcycles as a means of transporting troops.

One of the early proponents of motorcycles for delivering dispatches was Lieut Albert H. Trapmann of the 26th Middlesex (cyclist) Volunteer Reserve Corps, who in March 1907 argued against the suggestion of using motorcycles for transporting "man armed with a rifle", but suggested there was a role for motorcycles in the dispatch of signals. To the casual observer this action could be viewed as an attempt to safeguard the future of pedal cycles. But Trapmann, was a forward thinking military strategist[10] and an expert on military cycling. Far from seeing the motorcycle as a threat he was quick to spot an appropriate role. He wrote:

"It is useless for scouting, because its advent can be heard afar off; its weight and general unhandiness make it cumbersome to turn round in a narrow road or bypath: it cannot be lifted over hedges and stiles, nor dropped in a ditch; and, like all mechanically-propelled vehicles, it is not even always reliable, and some varieties and individual machines are difficult to start.

Now, all these things are essential for cycle that is to carry a man armed with a rifle into the firing line. There are also several other disadvantages under which the motorcycle labours from a military point of view. It would, for instance, be exceedingly difficult for even a small squad - say ten men - to ride along a road in anything like a military- formation or to "keep station."

The motor cycle has a far more important (and interesting) part to play than merely carrying a man and his rifle into the firing line, and it reaches the acme of its utility when it is employed in conjunction with the most mobile troops that exist - cyclists."

---

[10] Cyclists in Action, Foster Groom & Co, 1904.
The Military Cyclist's vade mecum, Foster Groom & Co, 1904.

He went on to champion the use of motorcycle Despatch Riders to link up Units. Saying:

"Each commander of a cyclist company should have at his disposal two motor cyclists to keep himself in touch with the four sections, his company, and also to keep in touch with the neighbouring companies on his right and left." [11]

Trapmann gave an example of an exercise in 1906 during which a motorcyclist was able to take a dispatch from cyclists who were exhausted after a sixty mile march and deliver it to headquarters via a long route skirting enemy lines.

From April 1908, the 26th later re-named 25th (County of London) Cyclist Battalion continued to use motorcyclists as Despatch Riders. These arrangements were echoed in other parts of the country, but these ad hoc activities proved to be unsatisfactory because of the shortage of volunteers.

Lobbying by organisations such as the Auto Cycle Union (ACU) and the press called for a reserve of motorcyclists to be used as part of a national defence force. In July of 1909 an initiative by the Motor Union resulted in the War Office accepting a small number of motorcyclists and machines, with military experience to join the September Cavalry manoeuvres as Despatch Riders. The War Office stressed that this was purely experimental. The riders were provided with quarters and were paid for expenses and petrol.

The 1909 Cavalry Manoeuvres held in the Oxford Area were reported to be a success. At least six riders took part riding their own Rex, Triumph, Singer, Moto-Reve and Zenith motorcycles.[12]

The success of the 1909 experiment led to a much larger scale exercise in August 1910 when volunteer riders were employed as vehicle escorts, scouts and Despatch Riders.

---

[11] Trapmann AH, Motorcyclists in Warfare, The Motor Cycle, 13 March 1907, P202
[12] The Motor Cycle, 27 October 1909, P824 Photograph

One of the volunteer motorcycle Despatch Riders described his experiences of the end of the exercise:

"From the top of this hill the scene of the operations baffles description : away below from Swallowcliffe to Compton Chamberlayne, the country looked like a map, with line upon line of infantry advancing to the attack, cavalry manoeuvring behind them, and then the artillery. On the hill were the Howitzer Batteries, Maxims, heavy guns, infantry, and the Canadians; from time to time roars of cheering would be heard as a line of skirmishers charged at the hill. The scene was brilliant : Sir John French with his escort in review order, the chief umpire with his staff, the Duke of Connaught, Lord Roberts, Sir Evelyn Wood, the Military Attaches in their wondrous uniforms, the thousands of troops, the booming of guns, the cheering—all added to the grandeur of a magnificent spectacle. At 5 p.m. the three blue balloons were sent up, signifying that the 1910 manoeuvres were over." [13]

Rider with a Minerva at Rowlands Castle during 1910 Manoeuvres

As a result of this experiment the Army Council announced the formation of a Technical Reserve to be made up of riders with their own motorcycles, willing to make themselves available for manoeuvres and in the case of national emergency. This development would formalise the growing number of unofficial groups already in existence such as the Auto Cycle Legion formed by motoring organisations to support in the defence of the country if required.

---

[13] The Motor Cycle, 27 October 1910, P1038

Despite positive feedback from the War Office, it transpired that the Army Council's idea of a technical reserve was no more than a list of names, which fell well short of the campaigners' wishes.

Albert (now Captian) Trapmann and others were continuing to use the Motor Cycle magazine to advertise for volunteer Despatch Riders and make the case for a more organised corps in the regular army.

Following the 1910 summer manoeuvres the War Office formed a Special Technical Committee to investigate how motorcyclists could be recruited. The Committee chaired by Director of Recruiting and Organisation, Brigadier General F.R.C Carleton included War Office personnel as well as Civilians including The Reverend F.W. Hassard-Short of the Automobile Association (AA) and Mr F. Straight of the Auto-cycle Union (ACU). Their report published on 5 December 1911 recommended the standards for numbers of personnel, pay, equipment and mechanical inspection of motorcycles[14].

Despite these apparently positive developments Trapmann and his compatriots felt that things had stalled. As we will see later The War Office were in fact acting with due diligence, considering carefully the implications of the Carlton recommendations in the context of the "Bigger Picture"; specifically the mammoth task of considering mechanised Cavalry Support. However, Trapmann who had been here before as a pioneer of cyclist battalions, and driven by a strong belief that motorcycles were a key part in the defence of the nation took matters into his own hands.

Early in 1912 he was the architect of The National Association of Cyclist Defenders later to become The Legion of Cyclists. The Legion of Cyclists was on the face of it a group of patriotic men, keen for a bit of excitement. To Trapmann and his fellow like-minded Officers it was a powerful lobby group that would convince the War Office of the need to implement his suggestion of a motorcycle Technical Reserve, and the recommendations of the Carleton Committee. This "protest" was to be achieved by a mass mobilisation of the Legion on 27 April 1912.

---

[14] Report of The Advisory Committee on Motorcyclists (Technical Reserve), 1911, National Archives: Ref WO33/3026

Postcards were sent out to the 173 members of whom 99 reported to Daventry in the Midlands. Once there they listened to a talk by General Alexander Thorneycroft about the importance of motorcycles in modern warfare, before competing in a Hill Climb Trial.

Frustrated at only 200 motorcyclists being allocated under the newly formed Territorial Army arrangements, Trapmann's Legion continued to advertise for members and by May they had reached the target of the 2,000 they felt necessary for the defence of the country. A second mobilisation exercise was announced for 9 June when 159 motorcyclists attended an event in Maidenhead.

It seems that Trapmann may have been achieving his goal as the third mobilisation exercise was to be the last. Shortly after the exercise in July the War Office announced that 255 motorcyclists would be required to support the annual manoeuvres in September. The allocation was: 80 drawn from the ACU, AA and Motor Union, 40 provided by the Cyclists Union, 70 from Cyclist Battalions, 20 from the Regular Army, 15 from the Officer Training Corps and 30 from the Special Reserve/Royal Engineers.

Trapmann checks Papers at Maidenhead   (Demaus Transport Photographics)

War Bike: British Military Motorcycling 1899-1919

As we will explore in the next chapter, this apparent renewed interest by the War Office was because the 1912 manoeuvres had provided the first opportunity to test the Army's new Mechanical Transport System. Trapmann's frustration and further mistrust of the War Office at this time may also relate to an application to the War Office in 1908 by the Territorial Cycle Battalion for Machine Gun transport in case of mobilisation[15]. Despite the fact that Cycle Battalions had experimented with motor cycles in 1899 and Tri Cars supplied by Autocariers Ltd (AC) in 1911[16], The Mechanical Transport Committee had taken four years to conclude that Hiring a Taxi Cab would be more efficient than use of a Motorcycle or Tri-Car.[17] It is clear that whilst the part-time reservists were keen to have the latest mechanical transport, The Mechanical Transport Committee saw the problem as one of transport to a fixed point rather than travelling in convoy. After lengthy consideration and consultation The Mechanical Transport Committee felt that the cycle column would not be able to keep up with a Tri-Car. They also considered that the rapid development of mechanical transport could lead to a high replacement costs.

Following the September Manoeuvres Trapmann and the other lobbyists were able to declare a victory as the Territorial Force motorcycle establishment was increased to: 112 for the Royal Engineers and 221 for Cyclists Battalions. These were to be volunteers between the age of 17 and 36 providing their own motorcycle for a term of four years. Motorcyclists were required to attend for 40 hours service in year one followed by 10 hours in subsequent years. An annual camp allowance of £6.6 shillings per day was paid together with a petrol and insurance allowance of 8 Shillings whilst on manoeuvres plus a further 8 Shillings if lodgings were not provided. Those attached to Cyclists Battalions also benefited from a £1 per year cycle grant and any damage sustained on duty made good.

---

[15] 9/GEN. No/889, The Mechanical Transport Committee Annual Report 1908, P9, Royal Logistics Corps Museum Ref: RLCA 5813
[16] The Motor Cycle, 18 August 1911, P777
[17] 9/GEN. No/889, The Mechanical Transport Committee Annual Report 1911/2, P11, Royal Logistics Corps Museum Ref: RLCA 5816

Trapmann, having played a pivotal role in the concept of the Despatch Rider disappears from the pages of the motorcycling press having begun a new campaign as a Special Military Correspondent during the First Balkan War[18].

During the early 1900's The British Army was a complex organisation consisting of The Regular Army and a myriad of volunteer forces.

In July 1913, following the establishment of an organised Territorial Reserve; Army Order No: 230 set the Carleton Committee recommendations in place establishing three classes of reserve military motorcyclists:

Class 1- *An organised Motor-cyclist Section of the Royal Engineers Special Reserve with detachments attached to a Signal Unit of the Royal Engineers for the purposes of administration and training. For service with the Expeditionary Force at Home or Abroad Establishment 11 Officers 136 Other Ranks including allowance for wastage during conflict (Rank of motor-cyclist not less than Corporal)*

Class 2- *A Territorial Reserve Force for service at Home with Motor-cyclists enlisted into the arm of the Service of the Units to which they are to be posted. Establishment - for Yeomanry Regiments Signal Units and Cyclist's Battalions Other Ranks 678 – for Signal Service of Fortresses and defending ports – 2 Officers. 124 Other Ranks (Rank of motor-cyclist not less than Lance Corporal (Unpaid).*

Class 3- *A Technical Reserve to act as a pool to easily replace vacancies or casualties arising during emergencies, manoeuvres or general mobilisation in Classes 1 and 2.*

Recommendations regarding the formation of Local Motorcyclist Reserve Committees to deal with recruitment and mobilisation were also put in place, and as we will see in the next chapter the War Office were also establishing motorcycles as an effective tool for the Regular Army and Royal Flying Corps.

---

[18] Trapmann AH, The Greeks Triumphant, 1915, Foster & Groom

MILITARY MOTOR CYCLING NOTES

BY CELERITER

THE MOTOR CYCLIST RESERVE.

THE recent *communiqué* from the War Office, published in *The Motor Cycle* a few issues ago, roughly outlined the scheme under which motor cyclists may join the army, but we are now enabled to give details regarding the matter.

As regards the London district, officers have been appointed to form the Motor Cyclist Reserve Committee.

Alternatives.

There are two schemes under which motor cyclists may serve their country.

Class I.—Motor cyclists required for duty with units of the Army Signal Service, Expeditionary Force.

Class II.—Motor cyclists required for service with units of the Territorial Force. While, in addition to the above, a motor cyclists' section (special reserve) has been formed of the Royal Engineers.

Before going into details representing each of these three classes, it is necessary to deal with the matter generally. In order to provide the necessary organisation for finding the *personnel* required, it has been decided to form committees in the different commands in Great Britain and Ireland.

Twelve committees will be formed, one in each Territorial Divisional Area in England and Wales. In Scotland there will be three committees. In Ireland two committees will be formed. The committees are to be composed of one or more military officers appointed by the general officer commanding-in-chief, preference being given where possible to officers having a knowledge of motor cycles; representatives of the principal motor cycle unions or associations in the districts, and, where necessary, representatives of the county associations. A military member and representative of a county association (if serving) will act as joint secretaries.

Special Requirements.

Candidates desirous of joining must have their motor cycles inspected and fill in the required certificate on an Army form. The certificate will then be passed in the case of a candidate for the Special Reserve to the officer in charge of the Royal Engineer Records, and in the case of a candidate for the Territorial Force to an officer of the Territorial Force Association of the committee. In the case of a special reservist the candidate must be medically examined.

As regards the Royal Engineers, Special Reserve, Motor Cyclist Section, the following arrangements have been approved.

In peace each detachment is attached to a unit of the Army Signal Service. For the purpose of administration and mobilisation the Motor Cyclist Section will be under the officer in command of the Royal Engineer Records. Officers will not be promoted above the rank of lieutenant.

Terms of Service.

The conditions and terms of service for officers will be similar to those laid down for Royal Engineers, Special Reserve. Their probationary training will consist of fifteen days' continuous training, to include pistol exercises and practices, with the regular signal unit to which they are attached. The annual training will consist of fifteen consecutive days' training, while officers may, in addition, with their own consent, be employed on military duty with the unit to which they are attached, or with any regular Special Reserve or Territorial Force unit. The officers will wear uniform of the Royal Engineers' pattern, and, in addition, will provide themselves with drab waterproof overalls, brown gauntlets, and goggles of a suitable description for use with motor cycles. They will be armed and equipped as mounted officers of the Royal Engineers with the exception of sword, saddlery, and spurs. The pay during training for special service will be the same as an officer in their rank in the Royal Engineers, Special Reserve. They will also draw the motor cycle allowance and travelling allowance under certain conditions. A certificate of proficiency at their trade will be required of men before their enlistment to fill vacancies as motor cycle artificer-corporals. Recruit training will be not less than seven nor more than fifteen days' continuous training. The annual training will be the same as for officers. Non-commissioned officers of the Motor Cyclists' Section, when training or on special service, will draw the same allowance as non-commissioned officers of corresponding rank in other branches of the Royal Engineers. Motor cycle artificer-corporals will receive pay at the rate of three shillings per day.

Expenses.

To cover the cost of petrol and wear and tear, and all liability for damage, an allowance of 8s. per day will be granted. Travelling allowance: Motor cyclists when joining for annual training or other military duty will, if they proceed by motor cycle, receive an allowance at the rate of 1½d. per mile, provided they travel by the shortest route and that the allowance does not exceed the expenses, first-class for officers and third-class for a man, which would have been incurred had they proceeded with their motor cycles by rail. Officers and other ranks will be required to submit their motor cycles for inspection before being permitted to join the Motor Cyclists' Section of the Royal Engineers, Special Reserve, and a further annual inspection will be carried out in the spring of each year. These inspections will be arranged for by the Motor Cyclist Reserve Committee of the district in which the motor cyclist resides. Penalties have been instituted for those who fail to turn up for inspection with their machines, or if the machines are not in a serviceable condition when inspected.

Mobilisation.

On receiving an order to mobilise, motor cyclists will report where ordered, bringing with them their machines fully equipped. Each motor cycle will then be inspected by the officer to whom the motor cyclist has had orders to report himself, who may take it over at a valuation or replace it by a new one. The motor cyclist must state the original price of the machine and the date of purchase, and produce a receipt, etc. On the motor cycle being taken over by the Government a reduction of 10% of the original cost will be made for the first year since purchase, and a further reduction of the original cost for each subsequent half-year or part thereof. The price paid will not be less than 30% of the original cost of the motor cycle.

Half the above equipment will be provided by the War Department and the rest must be provided by the motor cyclist himself.

Types of Machine.

Motor cycles must be of a well-tried and approved make, of which adequate stocks of spare parts are available in the country. They must be fitted with variable speed gear and magneto ignition. The wheels must be 26in. in diameter, with not less than 2¼in. tyres, for machines with engines of 500 c.c., and not less than 2in. tyres for machines with engines of 350 c.c. Engines to be single-cylinder of about 500 c.c., with dimensions of not less than 84 mm. bore and 84 mm. stroke. A certain number of horizontal twin-cylinder machines will be accepted. The magneto must be efficiently protected from the wet, and preferably of the waterproof type. The magnetos should, where possible, have interchangeable base and drive. Spring forks must be fitted, and the screw threads used should be standardised as far as possible. Lamps and generator to be fitted with brackets

The Motorcycle Magazine announces the arrangements for the Territorial Reserve.

3: War Office Procurement

In 1900 the War Office formed The Mechanical Transport Committee (MCT). It included four sub-committees: Experiment and Motor, Royal Artillery, Royal Engineers and Army Service Corps (ASC). The committee was responsible for exploring every aspect of transportation for the Army's supply train. At the outset their focus was mainly on steam, but broadened in scope to consider Motor - Lorries, Ambulances and later, Cars and Motorcycles.

In late 1907 early 1908 A.W. Wall of Birmingham supplied their 4 hp military model motorcycle to the War Office for evaluation. One was subsequently provided to Capt. A. Arkell-Hardwick, F.R.G.S., commanding the motor cycle section of the London Command of the Legion of Frontiersmen. This may have in turn lead to a contract to supply one machine to the Governor of Uganda. The motorcycle, which appears to the modern eye unsuitable for military use, faded away during 1910.

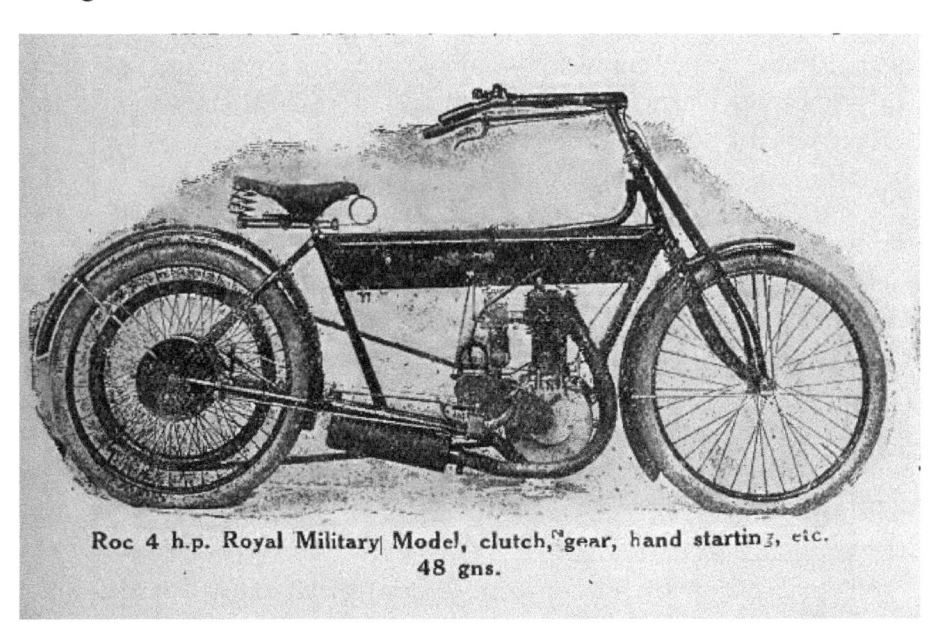

Roc 4 h.p. Royal Military Model, clutch, gear, hand starting, etc.
48 gns.

The 1908 ROC Military Model

War Bike: British Military Motorcycling 1899-1919

The MTC included as a member, Colonel Henry Holden, designer of the Brooklands race circuit and developer of the Holden motorcycle. Nevertheless, motorcycles remained very low on the MTC agenda. On 2 March 1908 the MTC considering an application from H & A Dufaux Ltd[19] to be placed on a list of motorcycles for consideration stated:

"It is understood that Motor Cycles are not generally suited for Mechanical Transport work".[20]

In 1909 Lorries and Motorcycles were officially used for the first time in manoeuvres and led to the formation of the Motor Vehicle Subsidy Scheme, whereby private vehicle owners would provide vehicles to the Army during mobilisation.

As discussed earlier, 1910 was a turning point. The 1910 Manoeuvres provided the first opportunity to test the use of motorcycles in the field. Despite some difficulty in obtaining the numbers required, the exercise demonstrated that motorcycles would enable officers to supervise motor lorry transport under their command and more significantly, in a way not possible by horse or cycle.

The 1910 Manoeuvres were generally regarded as a success and paved the way for the replacement of existing methods of supply, as a result General Haig recommended the organisation of a signals squadron of Cars and Motorcycles,[21] The MTC strongly recommended that motorcycles be used in all Mechanical Transport Companies to assist in proper communication. The MTC even hinted at the possibility of the use of motorcycles to transport troops, although this avenue was subsequently not pursued further until machine gun carriers were considered in 1914.[22]

---

[19] French Manufacturer of Motosacoche Motorcycles established in England as H & A Dufaux England Ltd
[20] Mechanical Transport Committee Annual Report 1908/9, P55, Royal Logistics Corps Museum Ref: RLCA 5813
[21] Winton G, Theirs not to Reason Why: Horsing the British Army 1875 – 1925, P198

Short of funds the MTC were able to purchase one Triumph 3½ hp motorcycle for evaluation before the end of the financial year.[23]

Recognising the enormous task of mechanising the British Army the MTC choose to supplement their own work by observing and reporting on each of the Auto-Cycle Union motorcycle trials[24]. This enabled the committee to observe a range of motorcycles under extreme conditions, leaving resources for testing more specialised machinery. This practice was to set the benchmark for subsequent reporting of the performance and development of motorcycles until the beginning of WW1.

Whilst the MTC had confidence that the motorcycle had a military future, they were keen to establish a set of standards for suitable motorcycles and arrangements for mobilising a force of civilian volunteers. These issues were addressed by The Carleton Committee during 1911 and annexed to the MTC Annual Report of 1911/12[25]

After an initial evaluation of the 3½ hp Triumph the MTC attended the Motorcycle Show at Olympia during November 1911 and later the same year purchased a 2¾ hp Douglas motorcycle.

The MTC had chosen motorcycles they felt represented the average lightweight and medium motorcycles available for the time. Their choices were also supported by choosing two manufacturers with a long standing presence in the marketplace. These manufactures would, after a lot of testing go on to supply the majority of the Army's motorcycles.

It is interesting to note that Douglas almost faltered at the first hurdle. The lightweight 2¾ hp fore and aft twin speed Douglas struggled even during the first evaluation. The manufactures were perhaps saved by a sympathetic MTC and the fact that they were quickly able to cure the problems.

---

[22] Mechanical Transport Committee Annual Report, 19010/11, P11/12, Royal Logistics Corps Museum Ref: RLCA 5815
[23] Mechanical Transport Committee Annual Report 1910/11, P6, Royal Logistics Corps Museum Ref: RLCA 5815
[24] 20 April 1910, 18 Aug 1910, 12 Oct 1910, 28 Jan 1911 and 22 April 1911
[25] Mechanical Transport Committee Annual Report, 19011/12, P54 Royal Logistics Corps Museum Ref: RLCA 5816

Douglas updated its engine to include a mechanically operated inlet valve enabling the machine to be more easily manoeuvred in traffic.

Looking back it does seem slightly strange that the lightweight Douglas was the eventual winner in the procurement process. However, at this stage the MTC were mainly concerned with cost and finding a machine suitable for those supervising convoys at low speed. An additional and significant factor in Douglas's favour was they were already contracted to supply generators, meaning mechanics could potentially service and maintain motorcycles as well as generators at a time when experienced Army mechanical engineers were at a premium.

The MTC considered the information from the 1911 Olympia Show together with the regular data from ACU events to arrive at a short-list. They then commenced full scale trials of motorcycles which began by inviting Royal Enfield, Douglas, Bradbury, P&M, Rudge and Premier to the Brooklands Race Circuit in Surrey on 29 January 1912.

Members of the MTC attending included Colonel H.C.L. Holden, now Committee President, R.A., Major O'Donohue A.S.C., Major Stevenson R.E., Captain H.E. Davidson R.E. (Secretary of the Committee), Major Cumberlegge A.S.C and Mr.Phelps of the India Office reviewed the motorcycles against the following standard:

- *40 mph for machines up to 350cc;*

- *45 mph for machines up to 500cc;*

- *Take a 12 Stone man up Test Hill from a standing start.*

On a cold winter day, with some areas of the Surrey race-track covered with frozen water from recent flooding, riders were asked to complete a circuit of the race-track from standing-start followed by a second lap after a flying-start. The machines were also run up the Test Hill, but unfortunately they were unable to weigh the men and machines as the equipment was flood-damaged.

Members of the Mechanical Transport Committee observe the January 1912 Trial

(Brooklands Museum)

Contemporary reports provide unofficial results after which The Motorcycle Magazine announced Zenith were the only entrants to have met the standard.[26] The magazine later apologised to Douglas Bros and Gibson the Bradbury Rider after they both disputed the claim.[27]

Following the session Douglas, P & M, Rudge, Premier, Triumph and Zenith received orders for the following motorcycles[28] for further testing on Salisbury Plain and Brooklands during 1912 to 1913. The machines supplied were:

- 2 x Rudge 3½ hp single gear Belt driven
- 1 x Premier 3½ hp 2 speed gear Belt driven
- 2 x P&M 3½ hp 2 speed gear Chain driven
- 1 x Douglas 2¾ hp 2 speed clutch model
- 1 x Douglas 2¾ hp 2 speed without clutch

---

[26] The Motor Cycle, 1 February 1912, P129
[27] The Motor Cycle, 8 February 1912, P143
[28] The Mechanical Transport Committee Annual Report 1911/12, P7, Royal Logistics Corps Museum Ref: RLCA 5816

War Bike: British Military Motorcycling 1899-1919

- 1 x Zenith 3½ hp Variable gear Belt driven

- 1 x Triumph 3½ hp single gear Belt driven

Zenith were soon claiming to be War Office Contractors and Oil Company Wakefield lost no time in using the Brooklands' tests to prove the virtue of their Castrol oil but it was Douglas that won this round of procurement.

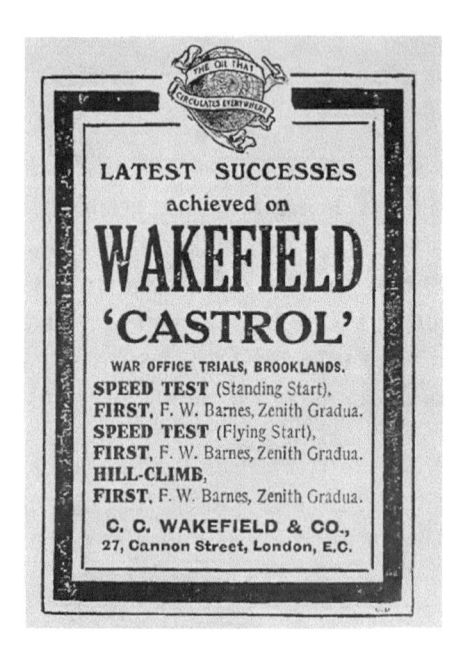

During the period 1911/12 the MTC also tested Bucket seats and Mud screens for motorcycles. The MTC had also considered the Carleton Committee's recommendations which established the three classes of motorcyclist, ranks, motorcycle standards, and tools to be carried.[29]

The Royal Flying Corps (RFC) were very 'late to the party'- having been formed in May 1912- remained untainted by the Horse vs Mechanical Transport argument. But, at a time when manned flight was a fairly new concept there were still some 'bridges to cross'.

Whilst initially there was debate at the War Office about the need for aircraft in modern warfare, the head of RFC's experimental work and first person to make a parachute jump from an airship in 1913 was in no doubt: Major Herbert Musgrave, being witness to the Blériot landing in a monoplane after the first flight across the English Channel in 1909, immediately saw the risk posed by fixed wing aircraft[30].

The RFC military wing also recognised, as a result of detailed experimentation by Musgrave, that there was a need for motor vehicles

---
[29] The Mechanical Transport Committee Annual Report 1911/12, P54, Royal Logistics Corps Museum Ref: RLCA 5816
[30] Raleigh W, The War In The Air, 1922,

to support piloted aircraft. Writing in advance of the conflict Lieutenant Barrington-Kennett wrote:

"There should be oil lorries for the distribution of petrol, and leather tool-bags to be carried on motor-bicycles to the scene of an engine break-down."[31]

Major Herbert Musgrave's meticulous work had led to the development of a detailed plan involving the deployment of RFC reconnaissance squadron including motorcycles, as support to an expeditionary force.

The RFC assessment of motorcycles was carried out by under the auspices of the War Office Mechanical Transport Committee.

Phelon and Moore (P&M) were discreetly asked by the War Office to provide three motorcycles for testing at the Brooklands Race Circuit in Surrey. Proud to be selected, they duly complied, only to find that Royal Enfield, Douglas, Premier, Zenith, Triumph, Bradbury and Rudge had also been asked. By the final RFC trial on 28 February 1913 only Douglas and P&M were being considered. Bertie Marians of P&M took personal responsibility for the batch of Eight 3½ hp Machines delivered to Brooklands, whilst Douglas provided 12 Model 'O' machines.

The trial consisted of the standard 50-mile dash around the oval circuit followed by a run up Test hill.[32]

Brooklands Test Hill

---

[31] Barrington-Kennett B, What I learnt on Manœuvres, 1913 Essay,
[32] Jones BM, The Story of Panther Motorcycles, Panther Publishing 2009, P37

War Bike: British Military Motorcycling 1899-1919

Once again the Douglas machines failed to impress and it was P&M that won the first significant contract. On Jan 1914 the War Office placed what was for the time the largest ever order: 20 x 3½hp machines. This RFC machine was essentially a 1914 Colonial model designed to cope with rugged conditions. By 1915 the Phelon & Moore Catalogue proudly stated they were exclusive suppliers to the Royal Flying Corps in France.

The Motorcycle Transport Committee felt that Douglas failed the trial as the Royal Flying Corps required a faster road speed. However, the ASC continued to be satisfied with Douglas and three more were ordered for the 1914/15 programme,[33] although many thousands more were subsequently required after outbreak of war.

A 1911 Phelon & Moore Colonial Model (Yesterdays)

---

[33] Mechanical Transport Committee Annual Report 1913/14, P54, National Archives Ref: WO107/285

4: The Clouds Gather

By 1914 the Mechanical Transport Committee established Triumph, Phelon & Moore and Douglas as preferred suppliers. The newly formed companies were not up to full peacetime complement, but the Committee were confident that Motorcycles could be readily obtained "over the counter" as required.

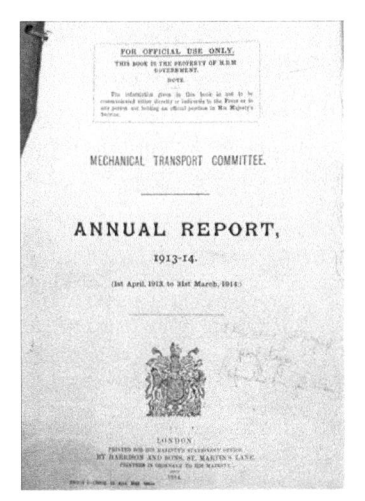

The Mechanical Transport Committee continued to review motorcycle developments by attending T.T. Races and ACU Trials; as a result a 6hp Zenith was identified but later found not suited for convoy work. However the concept & development of twin cylinder machines so impressed them it led to the purchase of a twin-cylinder 3¼ hp Lee-Francis, but the War halted reporting on the trial.

1913/14 MTC Draft Report Not Published   (Author)

The Committee showed interest in cycle-cars too, although the initial observations suggested they were unsuitable for military use and MTC trials of silencers followed resulting in all Douglas machines being fitted with the new pattern. This is perhaps further evidence of Douglas being able to respond quickly to change.

'The Motorcycle' magazine had regularly acted as a recruitment hub for civilian motorcycle riders to take part in army manoeuvres with their own machines; and the magazine offices were later listed by the War Office as a recruitment centre.

War Bike: British Military Motorcycling 1899-1919

ADVENTURES IN SCOTLAND
THE MOTOR CYCLE
Largest Net Sale. Founded 1903.
MOTOR BICYCLES – SIDECARS – CYCLE CARS
No. 588. Vol. 13. Thursday, July 2nd, 1914. Price 1d.

In annual manoeuvres motorcycles played a more important role; leading to establishment of the Motorcyclist Reserve Committees upon recommendation by the Carleton Committee; there were concerns however about lack of volunteer money paid and this affected the numbers according to correspondents: one volunteer wrote to the Motorcycle magazine complaining:

"... the rate of 8 Shillings per day did not compensate for wear and tear, and the increased insurance premiums' but views differed, another saying: 'My idea is that the annual camp work is one of the very best types of holiday that a motor cyclist can wish for"

The last quote is perhaps a more valid comment of perceived freedom and independence motorcycling affords, than first-step preparation for military action.

In 1913, any volunteer to the Special Reserve had to meet age criteria between 18-30 years and sign up for four years. It was stipulated a volunteer would receive:

- **During Training** - *2s. 6d. per day plus a mess allowance of 3d. per day, a ration allowance of 5d. per day, a clothing allowance of 6d. per day a motor cycle allowance of 8s. per day. In addition a travel allowance was paid at the rate of 1½d per mile for the shortest suitable route between their homes and the place of training.*

- **Married Men** - *received a separation allowance. Of 1s 1d for a Wife and 2d for each child.*

- *Bounties were paid, subject to annual motorcycle inspection, as follows:*
  - **Training** : *£1 received at end of training.*
  - **Non-training** ; *total of £4 per year.*

In 1915 these rates were the subject of continuing dissatisfaction, as prior to August 1914 serving members of the Territorial Army were being paid less than those who signed up post-mobilisation. The debate even reached Parliament: in a speech Sir John Spear said:

"I wish also to mention the case of the motor Despatch Riders in the Territorials, who have rendered great service. I know that in Devonshire we have had men who have become greatly experienced in motor despatch riding, these men are receiving 1s. 2d. a day, with two-pence towards their outfit, whereas if they had postponed joining and had joined Lord Kitchener's Army at the last moment they would now be getting 5s. a day for doing precisely the same work."[34]

The War Office had established the Army Transport Corps (ATC) and Mechanical Transport for the Royal Flying Corps. They set rudimentary standards for motorcycles, but remained reliant on reservists with their own machines in the case of mobilisation.

At this time, increasing debate followed in letters, columns and editorials about most suitable motor-cycle for military use: any motorcycles available at the time were still basically motorised bicycles; however, advances were claimed and manufacturers keen to aim their latest developments at the growing number of reservists.

By 1914 chain drives, multi-drive gears, hub brakes, and even electric starters had been developed, but the average bike was still a single cylinder belt-driven machine with little in the way of braking.

The entire stock of Mechanical Transport Committee motorcycles had been allocated to ATC Companies: these included motorcycles

---

[34] Hansard: HC Deb, 15 March 1915, Vol 70 column 1845-94

War Bike: British Military Motorcycling 1899-1919

purchased for testing as well as the preferred Triumph, Phelon & Moore and Douglas.

As tensions grew in Europe, other British Manufacturers had success with foreign military contracts. Royal Enfield sent 65 x 3 hp models to their Dutch importer just prior to the Dutch mobilisation - although there is no direct evidence of a military contract, they were used by the Dutch Army at the time of mobilisation in July 1914.

At the same time 15 x 3 hp. models were sent to the Royal Enfield Russian importer: photographic sources suggest these may have been part of a military contract; or an evaluation prior to a much larger contract.

On Saturday 20 June 1914, the Red Cross organised a Field Day to test Red Cross Volunteer Aid Detachment's (VAD) readiness for warfare: held at Brooklands Race Circuit[35], the test included use of a newly-conceived motorcycle ambulance[36] based on a Triumph with converted Gloria sidecar.

Triumph Gloria Ambulance at the 1914 Red Cross Field Day

---

[35] The Times, 22 June 1914 P22. Flight Magazine 12 June 1914 P618 & 26 June 1914 P683-684

[36] The Motor Cycle, 2 July 1914, P7

5: Mobilisation August 1914

The war in Europe was underway in July 1914, and the motorcycle press were reporting stories of motorcyclists caught in Europe as hostilities erupted. At first Britain seemed reluctant to become involved; however, the Belgian Alliance meant involvement was inevitable after Germany's invasion of Belgium.

On 4 August 1914 Britain declared war on Germany and on the afternoon of 5 August telegrams were sent to motorcycle manufacturers by the War Office requesting urgent supply of motorcycles for the army[37]. These 11,638 machines were immediately dispatched to agreed locations; and in just a few days were made available to troops leaving for France or training.

The Motorcycle magazine, published on 6 August, carried a report of its own correspondents having to 'make a dash' through France after postponement of the Grenoble International Six Day Trial. In the same edition under a simple heading **"War!"** The magazine wrote:

"At the moment of writing it appears that motor cyclists may soon find opportunities to show that their favourite sport is more than a healthy and instructive hobby. They may be called upon in large numbers to put their knowledge, machines, and even lives at the disposal of the country. The equipment which has provided many a day's sport and many an evening's discussion will be at the free disposal of fellow countrymen. Let us trust that we shall be found useful if our services are required. The lives which many of us have often risked for sport and commerce in the past will be more readily offered in a sterner cause"

Motorcyclists were urged to volunteer to the magazine offering their services: however, this well intentioned plea (written as the publication was going to press) contradicted instructions for volunteers to report to

---

[37] Clew J, The Douglas Motorcycle: The Best Twin, P50

[38] Statistics of the Military Effort of the British Empire, P877, British Library Ref: 9085.h.13.

their nearest recruitment centre, and may have led to volunteers missing out on the first recruitment drive.

APPENDIX B.

PLACES OF JOINING FOR REGULAR RESERVISTS.

Branch.	Place of joining.
Cavalry	Cavalry depôts.
R.H.A.†	R.H.A. depôt.
R.F.A.†	R.F.A. depôts, as ordered by the officer i/c R.H. and R.F.A. records.
R.G.A.†—	
Reservists allotted to coast defences	As ordered by the officer i/c R.G.A. records.
Reservists not allotted to coast defences.	R.G.A. depôts, as ordered by the officer i/c R.G.A. records.‡
Mountain Artillery Reservists	R.F.A. depôt, Woolwich.
School of Gunnery	
Artillery Clerks Section	} No. 1 depôt, R.G.A., Newhaven.‡
R.E.—	
All except unallotted reservists	Place of mobilization of unit.§
Mounted reservists unallotted to units.	Training depôt for field units, R.E., Aldershot.
Dismounted reservists unallotted to units.	R.E. depôt, Chatham.
Royal Flying Corps (Military Wing)	Headquarters, R.F.C. (M.W.), South Farnborough.

Extract from The 1914 Mobilisation Regulations (Author)

Upon outbreak of the War the British Army owned just 80 mechanised vehicles including 15 Motorcycles[39], furthermore the regular army was based in India, Malta and other parts of the British Empire. The Military plan, which was in place to support an ally abroad, was brought into play.

The 1914 plan to counter German refusal to withdraw from Belgium, was to build a British Expeditionary Force consisting of Regular Army Companies and squadrons of the Royal Flying Corps, which now featured motorcyclists, drawn from the Special Reserve, for duties such as dispatch delivery, mechanical support and convoy support; but, this led to shortages. The location of suitable mechanical transport had been logged prior to the War and was immediately pressed into service, hence the pictures of troops seen on B-Type London Buses: over 1,000 were subsequently used.

---

[39] (Excluding the Royal Flying Corps) Statistics of the Military Effort of the British Empire, P852, British Library Ref: 9085.h.13.

Reservists had their motorcycles requisitioned and were sent across the Channel or to UK postings; volunteer motorcyclists responding to press articles were now turning up at recruitment centres. The War Office plan was any volunteer's motorcycle meeting the standard would be requisitioned and its owner paid full price for a 1914 machine or 10% less per year for those manufactured prior to 1914 (Subject to a minimum payment of 30%). Men who signed up as Despatch Riders were given the rank of Corporal, paid 35 Shillings a week and paid a £10 bounty. The length of their contract was specified as 12 months, or the duration of the War, and volunteers with sub-standard motorcycles were allocated new machines upon arrival at the training camp.

Immediate requisition of motorcycles was important to avoid any complications at a later stage, even though in theory an owner was more likely to keep their own machine well maintained, poor condition of the roads, lack of time and the inaccessibility of tools meant it was much more practical to re-issue new or refurbished machines than enter negotiations with an owner over motorcycle value in the Field

On occasion 'chancers' presented to the Recruitment Office attempting to make a few pounds: e.g. one gent turning up with a four year old motorcycle he valued at £35 unaware the Officer was an experienced motorcyclist, resulting in a prompt dismissal: asked repeatedly how he had the audacity to value a machine of un-determined vintage at such a high figure, the Officer tore his paper in half, and sent him about his business.

In August 1914 fear of invasion 'loomed' over Britain and therefore the mobilisation included reinforcement of the Territorial Force: this already included volunteer motorcyclists and the need for despatch riders for military HQ duties, and attachment to the Police Force increased. The Metropolitan Police employed 50 motorcycle mounted Special Constables and again they relied on riders to provide their own machines: and as unpaid roles each owner received 2d (two pence) per mile expenses. Special Constables including some on motorcycles were employed by Police Forces up and down the country.

Several pictures exist in the motorcycle press of this time featuring armed military personnel in East Anglia. One photo showed a detachment of Despatch Riders using a school and playground as temporary base and others riders being challenged by armed soldiers - this may have been part of a propaganda exercise to reassure people there was a high level of military presence but in reality the East Coast of England had been identified as an area of high risk; both from invasion as well as targeted attacks on vital Naval Signal Stations and Wireless Telegraph Stations in East Anglia.

Military Motorcyclists & Cyclists gather somewhere in East Anglia (Mortons)

The Home Defence Eastern Command Scheme - a classified document completed in 1913 - set out locations of vital strategic assets and means of defence, listing suitable areas from which London could be defended in the south and east during mobilisation: referred to as the Precautionary Period in the Plan, or after the British Expeditionary Force was in place: described as The War Period.[40] The Mobilisation Regulations[41] were used by local commanders when putting Home Defence Schemes in place. For example the regulations set out that a

---

[40] The Home Defence Eastern Command Scheme, National Archives Ref: WO33/671
[41] Mobilisation Regulations, National Archives Ref: WO33/3396

suitable type of buildings for billeting troops would be a (Day) school with playground for vehicles.

Cyclist Battalions feature in the Defence plans as a mobile force for defence and observation; as discussed earlier most of these battalions were now supported by motorcycles, for dispatches and transport of officers: in reality motorcycles were able to patrol a much larger area than the bicycle.

During the August Mobilisation, local Motorcyclist Reserve Committees issued repeated calls for volunteers to report to recruiting centres and Rallies around the country. Motorcyclists responded in large numbers and requirements were soon oversubscribed. Captain Albert Trappman returned from service abroad and was responsible for a Recruitment Centre in Putney, South London. He reported that he had 2,000 excess men within a few days. Those successful included 25 with language skills who were immediately pressed into service as interpreters; unsuccessful were encouraged to study map reading and Army conditions so they were better prepared if further vacancies occurred. As competitions were halted Motorcycle Cubs were asked to arrange map-reading competitions; some even introduced rifle practice!

One Recruitment Rally was held on Saturday 8 August at the Windmill, Wimbledon Common where 500 riders attended. This must have been a pre-arranged event as books were closed to motorcycle recruits: some motorcyclists were pictured proudly displaying their new "OHMS" plates on their Metropolitan Police issue motorcycles.

One hundred years on, the scale of this mobilisation is daunting: troops transported to ports by train, others were dispatched to various strategic locations across the country. At the last Brooklands Race Meeting reports say the crowd seemed more interested in Newsboys and Troop Trains alongside the railway, than any action on the track. Expeditionary Force Tables[42] listed Units to be mobilised and days by which they had to report for embarkation at the ports – subsequent annotations to this document with actual dates demonstrate the majority of the initial Force had sailed by 19 August.

---

[42] British Expeditionary Force Tables, National Archive Ref: WW33/606

Motorcyclists attached to the initial force consisted mainly of Special Reservists and those attached to The RFC. The BEF travelled through France into Belgium without experiencing any contact with enemy forces. Some have suggested German Generals were content to draw the BEF into Belgium before engagement, whilst Basil Thompson[43]- closely linked to the intelligence services - suggests the BEF was in the Field before the generals knew anything about it. It was an impressive feat to deliver 150,000 men, their Horses, vehicles and equipment to Belgium from numerous locations in Britain and Ireland.[44]

During this period the regular army relocated from India, and other British Colonies: one Motorcyclist Section sailed from Bombay on 24 August on the "Assaye" to Egypt arriving on 9 September. They were then held until 19 September before boarding the "Perugia" arriving at Marseilles on 26 September[45]. It would be late October 1914 before many of the regular Army units were available in the Field.

One Despatch Rider described travelling from Newcastle to Chatham in Kent to sign up to the Special Reserve and upon arrival men and machines were inspected; although this particular rider passed the medical, his own pride and joy, a 3½ hp 1912 Bradbury was found unsuitable for service and returned home at the Army's expense. meanwhile he obtained uniform, equipment and undertook basic training including, drill and map reading; duties included unpacking and assembling new Rudge-Multis and three-speed Triumphs, before riding his brand new machine to join his allocated Unit in Aldershot. This example demonstrates the pace at which things were moving, as they were unloading new bikes in Chatham just two days after War had been declared.[46]

---

[43] Sir Basil Home Thompson KCB, Assistant Commissioner (Crime) Metropolitan Police
[44] Thompson B, Queer People, 1922, Hodder & Stoughton, P35
[45] General Programme of Moves by Sea, 1914, National Archives: Ref WO33/708
[46] The Motorcycle Magazine, 10 Sept 1914, P314

6: Life on the Front Line

And so motorcycle works riders, including a few due to take part in the abandoned International Six Day Trial (6-9 August) were called back to their units or volunteered for service.

Vernon Busby, from a picture taken in 1913

One such person was Vernon Busby a prominent Sunbeam Rider of the time who had enjoyed a busy season: gaining success as part of the winning Sunbeam Team 1914 Isle of Man T.T., on 26 June he won five races at the Westcliffe Speed Trials; in July took part in The Midland Club's Cycle-car Trial driving a Morgan winning a Gold medal and for the Non-stop Run. He signed up in Birmingham on 10 August and landed in France on 16 August as a member of the Royal Engineers[47].

In a series of contemporary published pieces[48] he paints a vivid and surprisingly frank picture of the scene during the August mobilisation.

He, like our previous volunteer was asked to report to the Headquarters of the Royal Engineers at Chatham where there was just time for a few drills before being addressed by an officer who told them:

---

[47] Personnel Records of Captain Vernon Busby, National Archives Ref: WO339/25492
[48] The Motor Cycle, September 3, P302 & September 10, P333

War Bike: British Military Motorcycling 1899-1919

"*(They) would be engaged in the most dangerous work, and if half of their number reached England again they would be lucky.*"

As a member of a Signals Company Busby may have received additional training in Ireland, as he says he sailed from Ireland to France having to sleep on deck and eat biscuits and bully beef "*which to the civilian accustomed to the daily comforts of English home life, was exceedingly trying*". He explains how, riding his 3½ hp Sunbeam in mud almost up to the axles, the section had to stop every mile to let troops past. The detachment of 15 consisted mostly of Triumphs and Douglas machines, and one Rover; accompanied by their commanding officer, riding a Swift Cycle-car loaded with petrol tins. On one occasion it took 20 men to free the Swift from the mud. This slow progress continued until they were placed on a train close to the Belgian town of Mons.

Although the detail of his journey to the front had some place names redacted, the account is surprisingly candid - he describes '*German aeroplanes unfortunately accurately discovered the position of our troops*' He went on '*... matters got so serious that Motorcyclists had to go out in pairs, and were instructed to drive with one hand on the handle-bars and carry a revolver in the other.*'

Once they arrived at the front Busby was an Artificer Corporal in a Signal Station south west of Mons, and responsible for the wellbeing of the 17 motorcycles, including two spares allocated to their detachment. Their duties were to lay and maintain telegraph wires from the HQ to the forward lines.

In these early days, before stalemate of trench warfare, there was a lot of troop movement, and their duties also entailed cutting telegraph wires as the order to retire was given so the communications did not fall into enemy hands. Vernon Busby recounts how his detachment was tasked with locating lost columns on the move, as well as delivering dispatches.

In our present digital age of radio, mobile phones and SMS the challenge of maintaining communication to thousands of troops is hard to imagine; with the vehicles on the move, let alone communicating during the heat of battle. We know from reports of Military exercises in Southern England in June and July of 1914, Marconi Radios were used to transmit information from forward lines to the field telegraph posts. However, the generators presented mobility and overheating issues so the Motorcycle Despatch Rider was still considered the most reliable form of communication.

After 14 days at the front, Busby was struck by a bullet and on 30 August invalided back to England where he was able to tell his story: his Sunbeam motorcycle, now the property of the Army, was handed over to another rider. He recounts graphic stories of how several motorcyclists were killed in heavy fighting and how a doctor riding a Rudge was blown to pieces by a shell. This appears genuine journalistic reporting rather than being 'tainted' by propaganda. This level of detail, viewed as heroism in the early days, was to disappear as the war dragged on.

Another, more famous volunteer was William Watson author of Adventures of a Despatch Rider. His account was contemporary to events and published in 1915; representing his own story between August 1914 and February 1915.

Watson signed up with some pals from Oxford University: as linguists they hoped to join the Intelligence Corps, but like Busby he was sent to Chatham then to Dublin, embarking for Le Havre and onward to Mons. Corporal Watson's story is compiled from letters home revealing how his initial zest depleted after the rigours of War at the front, even from the privileged position of a Despatch Rider.

During the first few days riders are able to enjoy a freedom to eat and drink at les Cafes: highlighting the overall movements of troops during this period and the vital role played by the Despatch Rider in the field of War.

Watson describes the *'organised chaos'* of the advance as he and colleagues maintained communications until the Signal Office was established.

"In the course of my riding that day I knocked down a "civvy" in Dour, and bent a foot-rest endeavouring to avoid a Major, but that was all in the day's work"[49]

A description of mixed progress over the roads: it details regular breakdowns, which meant the Despatch Rider had to use his wits to get to his destination. Watson explains how after abandoning his bike in mud after his light failed, he made his way on foot, stopping at an Inn *"... to gorge on coffee, rum and a large sandwich"*.

He resumed his journey on foot; flagging down a French Staff car with the 'story' that he had an important despatch: swiftly taken to his destination in a warm, dry car he admits to the reader his pocket contained only a bundle of receipts.

Watson sums up his own feelings in October 1915; writing to a friend, Robert Whyte he says:

"I shall never be able to write "Alec and I" again—and he was the sweetest and kindest of my friends, a friend of all the world. Never did he meet a man or woman that did not love him. The Germans have killed Alec. Perhaps among the multitudinous Germans killed there are one or two German Alecs. Yet I am still meeting people who think that war is a fine bracing thing for the nation, a sort of national week-end at Brighton."[50]

The day after Watson had written this letter, he received news that Robert had also been killed.

The relative privilege of rank (plus in Watson's case good education and fluent French) and job description meant the average Despatch Rider was far better off than the men, including the officers, on the front line in the author' opinion.

This is further reinforced by Eustace Booth, a rider with the Army Service Corps.

---

[49] Watson WHL, Adventures of a Despatch Rider, 1915, Chapter 2,

[50] Watson WHL, Adventures of a Despatch Rider (Introduction), 1915, Letter to Robert Whyte.

He joined up in October 1914 and thought he would be back by Christmas. His story recounted in 1986[51] gives us a little more insight into the conditions on and near the front. He modestly describes himself as a glorified messenger boy loaned out to different sections. He would travel to the HQ to get orders and return. Sometimes he did not change his clothes for a week and had to kill the lice in the seams of his uniform; having to sleep in barns and dodging shells. He would often get to a cross road that was being shelled and have to work out the interval of the shells. He would rush across before the next shell landed. He explained he was lucky to escape after a shell brought down one of the walls of a barn he was sheltering in. Even after these experiences, stated that all of this was much better than being in the Trenches.

He describes how the landscape changed over time:

"The fields became mud and full of water, no green, all the trees were shot off. The Roads were very greasy, had to drive with my feet on the ground; very hard on the motorcycles. They only lasted for about six weeks before I had to get a new one. I drove into shell holes many times."

On one occasion he rode to Ypres to the town square there were many buildings on fire, the beams were smouldering in the wind, making them glow. He saw many dead horses and a gun team cutting the throat

---

[51] Booth ER, Imperial War Museum Interview Cat No: 9263

of an injured horse. Day-after-day of disturbing scenes and lucky breaks led inevitably to bouts of depression, but explained that the medical staff *"did not have much time for you unless you had your arm blown off"*. Eventually he snapped after a shell landed near him and he collapsed with exhaustion and "Shell Shock". He was sent back for treatment in Britain followed by six months home leave. His luck remained with him as the war ended before he had to return to the front.

Booth's memories reveal an altogether darker picture than the contemporary "Jolly Sporting" stories. Corporal F.A. Enders R.E. account of his time on a 3½ hp Phelon & Moore attached to the Cavalry in the heart of the action, clearly demonstrates both the excitement of the individuals and the need to attract more recruits. He describes riding as *"A continuous trial of the ACU brand"* and went on to say:

"motor cyclists are not used for scouting purposes, the noise of the exhaust of the engine obviously being a great drawback, but I can assure readers that the average rider will find enough excitement and thrilling episodes to satisfy his appetite in the daily duties of a Despatch Rider in France."[52]

This is a man who lies in hospital having been shot in the foot and received severe internal injuries after being kicked by a horse, before being transported in a Cattle Truck for three days, and on to Glasgow by Ship; adding that he is keen to receive orders to return to duty.

Further afield in Africa another Despatch Rider wrote about how on one journey he rode into a pack of large Baboons and saw two Leopards. This story originally printed in The Daily Mail and picked up by The Motorcycle magazine[53] was another example of the press stressing the excitement of the "overseas adventure".

---

[52] The Motor Cycle, October 15 1914, P445 & 22 October P464

[53] The Motor Cycle, 15 October 1914, P448

7: The Military Motorcycle in 1914

Vernon Busby describes how some machines were damaged by inexpert handling, yet his description of the difficulties of travelling along roads full of vehicles through either dust or deep mud would be challenging to contemporary road machines. The motor cycles used throughout the First World War were for all purposes recreational road-going, belt driven vehicles. Some may have been modified by their owners for trials riding and others were "Colonial" models modified by the manufacturers for continental touring, or possible use in the military market.

In August 1914 at the Declaration of War The Motorcycle Magazine published their idea of the ideal military motorcycle concluding the machine should be a light and powerful silenced 500cc twin speed, ideally V-twin with standard controls, chain drive, with large tank appropriate mudguards and good brakes; they deal at length with lighting recommendations kit, capacity and even the paint finish, stating it should be black enamel rather than nickel plated, with surprisingly no mention of ground clearance.

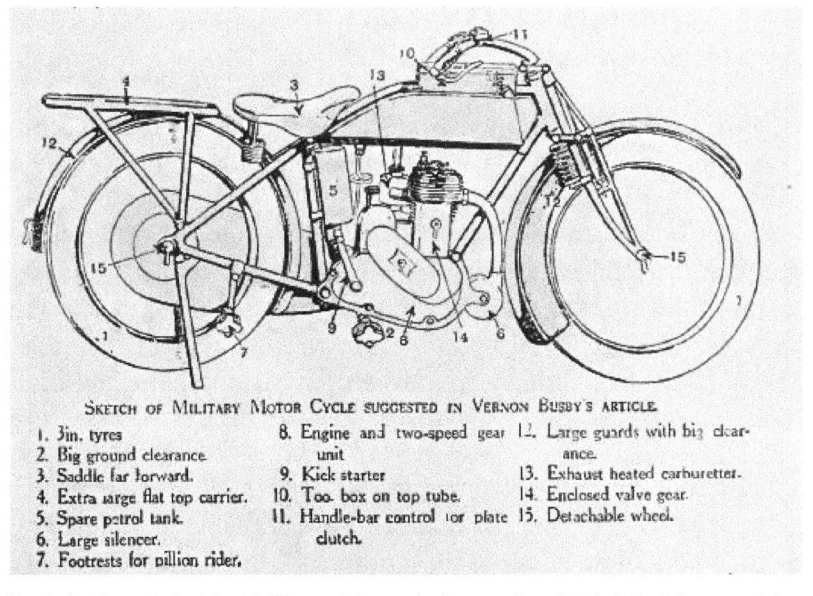

SKETCH OF MILITARY MOTOR CYCLE SUGGESTED IN VERNON BUSBY'S ARTICLE.

1. 3in. tyres
2. Big ground clearance.
3. Saddle far forward.
4. Extra large flat top carrier.
5. Spare petrol tank.
6. Large silencer.
7. Footrests for pillion rider.
8. Engine and two-speed gear unit
9. Kick starter
10. Tool box on top tube.
11. Handle-bar control for plate clutch.
12. Large guards with big clearance.
13. Exhaust heated carburetter.
14. Enclosed valve gear.
15. Detachable wheel.

Busby's idea of the ideal Military Mount in September 1914 (The Motorcycle)

Writing at the end of September (with the benefit of battlefield experience) Vernon Busby updated magazine readers with his version of the ideal military mount. He states that speed is not as important as a simple easily maintainable twin speed machine of 500cc to 600cc with the ability to run at average speeds of 40-50mph over 3,000 to 4,000 miles. He does mention it is essential to have good ground clearance; and in one article tending towards an advert for Sunbeam, mentions an enclosed chain drive and black paint: although as an ex-Sunbeam works' rider he stresses he is writing from personal experience of many different machines! Some other modifications suggest including a spare half-gallon tank, tool kit mounted on the main tank, exhaust heated carburettor, detachable wheels, a strong rack for kit and pillion footrests, to enable passengers if required.

The Government machine in August 1914 for Royal Engineers or Army Service Corps, was likely to be a single cylinder 4 hp Model A Triumph, or a twin cylinder 2¾ hp Douglas. Despatch riders attached to the Royal Flying Corps were supplied with single cylinder, chain driven 3½ hp P&M machines. These machines were a combination of fixed drive and geared machines, suggesting manufactures supplied whatever was available. The majority of later machines were supplied in military olive green although at the outbreak of war machines supplied were of a standard pattern, supplied with spare belt drives and boxes for tools mounted on the rear rack.

In 1915 Triumph supplied their first Model H, which was to become the synonymous as the WW1 "Trusty Triumph" motorcycle.

Just about every British motor cycle manufactured in 1913 and early 1914 had a German made magneto; ironically Triumph who supplied more machines than any other company was founded by German immigrants Siegfried Bettmann and Mauritz Johann Schulte. The reliability their machines were largely owed to the German Bosch magneto.

Although supplies of German made magnetos ceased causing a shortage. The War Office requisitioned all available supplies of Bosch magnetos, and almost certainly continued to obtain supplies from

American (then neutral) based factories. Whilst it was both impractical and morally unacceptable to rely on "enemy" parts, the British made magnetos did not meet the same standards of reliability as their German counterparts.

1914 Triumph Featuring a Bosh Magneto (Author)

The Motorcycle Magazine however was soon promoting magnetos by British manufacturers which could be retro-fitted in place of the Bosch model: including Thompson Houston (BTH), Morris & Lister, C. A. Vandervell and Co (CAV) and The Splitdorf Electrical Company.

All motorcycles at this time had rigid frames with the suspension provided by girder forks. The rider did have additional protection provided by a sprung saddle, however the full force of the road, anything from a muddy track to railway sleepers or Pavé (cobble stone)

War Bike: British Military Motorcycling 1899-1919

was transferred directly to the frame, resulting in many breakages. The only lighting was provided by acetylene lamps which soon expunged or rattled loose. Broken bike parts and mechanical breakdowns meant that changes of motorcycle were common resulting in regular change.

A recent photo of a Military Phelon & Moore Motorcycle in "original" condition
(Depositphotos.com)

8: Customisation & Standardisation

Many motorcycles were modified by riders to give additional protection to legs and engine from the mud and debris. Others had their hand-shift gear levers modified into foot-shifts and drop down T.T. style handlebars were fitted and later became standard on later versions of the Triumph Model H.

A guard manufactured in the Field to protect the magneto from mud
(Manx Aviation & Military Museum)

War Bike: British Military Motorcycling 1899-1919

Ever resourceful, riders were using ordnance to make parts. In 1917 a Douglas motorcycle was seen with polished plug protectors made from discarded shell cases! The rider said that prior to the modification he had been constantly stopping because thick wet mud was shorting out his plugs.

Top of an 18lb Shell made into a plug protector   (The Motor Cycle)

Other customisation was purely decorative; pennants and badges were common whilst other embellishments were more personal. Royal Engineers rider Albert Simpkin's diary entry for 9 April 1918 says:

'"Hob" says we should leave our motorcycles to their fate, but I have a great love for that machine, which I have fitted with all manner of gadgets, a polished copper exhaust pipe and a blue and white pennant on the front mudguard."[54]

---

[54] Venner D, Despatch Rider on the Western Front 1915-18: The Diary of Sergeant Albert Simkin MM, 2015, Pen & Sword, 2015

Customisation was not without hazard; not least because the rigid regulations demanded no motorcycles should be altered from their delivery specification; even as mudguards were removed following clogging, riders in many cases had to seek permission for modification. One rider stated permission was given by a senior officer to remove the front guard, and replace it with an arrangement of canvas whilst fashioning a rear guard from a canvas bag to ease the passage through the mud.

On other Fronts there were different challenges: desert riders found soft sand demanding, inevitably tempered by comments about the weather being *"much better than at home"* and *"... conditions those on the Western Front could only dream of!"*

As the flimsy frames and cycle parts 'fell victim' to the rugged terrain, it became more important that standardisation was introduced. The existing repair infrastructure was just not capable of repairing such a wide range of motorcycles.

Many of the requisitioned motorcycles became damaged beyond repair and more likely to be replaced by the Government standard Model H Triumph, Douglas or P&M.

BSA produced many thousands of bicycles for the war effort, but only a relatively small number of military motorcycles. These saw action in East Africa. Clyno became the standard machine gun carrier although Scott carriers and solos continued to be used in Gallipoli, perhaps due to their engines being water cooled and more able to cope with the hot conditions. Many other British manufacturers continued to supply allied forces. (See also Sidecars, Gun Carriers and Ambulances)

 With more standard machines in the Field, motorcycles could be repaired quickly using available spares. Non-standard models were returned to Britain for repair if spares were available and marked for 'Home use only'.

The Royal Flying Corps faced significant problems after choosing Phelon & Moore as their standard motorcycle, due to the lack of Phelon & Moore spares and expertise available in Army workshops.

War Bike: British Military Motorcycling 1899-1919

Mr Richard Moore was asked to intervene and, after several visits to the Western Front by him and other members of the company, Specialist Repair Shops were established enabling Phelon & Moore motorcycles to be repaired 'in the Field' or returned to workshops at home.

9: The War Years

1915 Developments

War brought frantic activity, constant rumours of spies and increased military presence on patrol around areas of strategic importance. On 19 January 1915 the first Zeppelin raids took place on the east coast towns of Great Yarmouth and Kings Lynn in Norfolk impacted on civilian morale; yet to many in Britain the war seemed distant and everyday life went on as normal.

The showcase for motorcycles was the annual motorcycle show at Olympia. The November 1914 show was cancelled as the venue was being used as a detention centre for German Aliens, but the motorcycling press had already reviewed the bikes and most new 1915 motorcycles were available to buy. Manufacturers were quick to use the War as a promotion tool and in days before advertising standards manufactures proclaimed the merits of models used by the military.

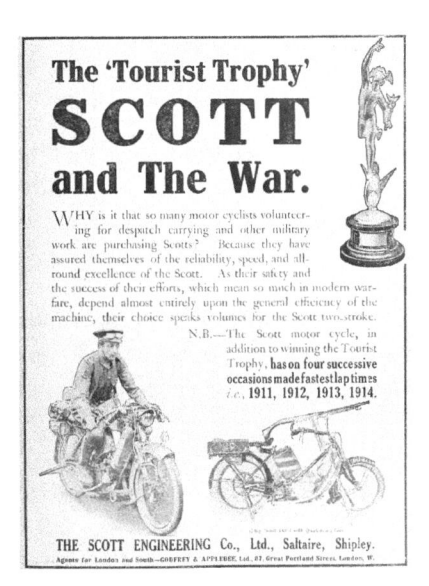

One example was the Scott, not yet under formal contract, who produced an advert with a picture of a soldier in uniform previously printed in The Motor-Cycle Magazine.

Manufacturers Triumph, P&M, Clyno and Douglas were supplying the War Office in large numbers and were celebrating the fact in full page adverts. P&M apologised to their potential customers for the delay in producing their catalogue due to the war effort and included testimonials from serving officers of the RFC.

It is difficult to imagine that civilian P&M motorcycles could have been available in any numbers, as by the end of 1915 the Royal Flying Corps and Royal Naval Air Service (RNAS) were receiving 40 machines a week from P&M. Additionally P&M were awarded a contract to supply 200 3½ hp machines to the Russian Imperial Army although subsequently suspended after only half of the original machines were supplied.

The Russians were forced to look to other manufactures as the P&M factory at Cleckheaton was put under Government control and subsequently moved to 24hr shifts to keep up with supply to The RFC.[55]

In 1915 Royal Enfield were unable to keep up with civilian motorcycle orders as they were supplying 500 bicycles a week to the War Office as well as regular orders to the Russian Government.

Throughout 1915 there were appeals for volunteers to sign up to the newly formed Motor Machine Gun Service (MMGS). Once again Motor Cycle Magazine took a leading role: requests were often followed by 'in the field' reports by volunteers. One such report - clearly designed with further recruiting in mind - quoted two rider's experiences at the Bisley Training Centre in Surrey:

"Just a line to thank you for helping me to join the M.M.G.S' I consider my joining about the best thing I have ever done. I have been in the Army now about six weeks, and like the open air life very much; in fact, it is a holiday, but we are being paid for it. The only thing I should like better is to be out in France with the boys, as no doubt we shall soon.

"You will be pleased to hear that I like the work very much, and certainly we cannot complain of being overworked. We knock off at 4 p.m., and can do what we like until 9.30 p.m. There is plenty of bathing, and I get a run on my Indian every day."

---

[55] Jones BM, The Story of the Panther Motorcycle, Panther Publishing 2009, P38

During 1915 weekly requests called for volunteers for the MMGS: suggesting the War Office was slow at meeting their aim of one Motor Machine gun Battery for each Division. (See also Sidecars)

In August 1915 some manufacturers - notably Phelon & Moore - were placed under Government Control; civilian production halted. Manufacturers no longer able to produce motorcycles were keen to let the public know they too were engaged in important war work: BSA, Rudge Whitworth and Raleigh produced large quantities of Bicycles, others produced munitions e.g. Chater Lea made taps for screwing on non-slip "roughs" to horse shoes.

A welcome distraction from military matters occurred in the summer, when two combined services motorcycle meetings were held at Brooklands. Manufacturers were quick to use the results to promote their motorcycles. (See also Competitions and Record Breaking)

This is Second Lieutenant Barnard and his

$3\frac{1}{2}$ h.p. Sunbeam.

He is holding the Cup presented him for scoring the most wins at the All-khaki Meeting at Brooklands, on August 7th.

His Sunbeam made both the slowest time of the day and the fastest on the test hill.

Catalogue on application to—

JOHN MARSTON, Ltd.,
11, Sunbeamland, Wolverhampton.

London Showrooms—57, Holborn Viaduct, E.C., and 157-158, Sloane Street, S.W.

Sunbeam Advert following the 1915 Brooklands All-khaki Meeting

Despite the drop in production the motorcycling press were reporting in September of more than 50 new British models and American imports for 1916. The 1915 Motor Cycle Magazine Buyers Guide even lists a motorcycle called "Despatch Rider" manufactured by Dreng Ltd of

War Bike: British Military Motorcycling 1899-1919

Fern Road Birmingham. This was a 2 H.P. single cylinder two-stroke which looked unsuitable for use in the field!

Despatch Rider.
2 h.p., 1-cyl., 2-stroke, 64 × 67 mm., 210 c.c. Ericson magneto. Amac carburetter. Single geared. Belt, ⅞in. Height 25in. Clearance 7¼in. Wheelbase 46in. Dunlop tyres, 24 × 2in. Drip feed. Petrol, 1¼ galls. Price £28 7s. Weight, 80 lb.
DRENG, LTD.,
Fern Road, Erdington, Birmingham.

The Dreng Despatch Rider Motorcycle from 1915 (The Motorcycle)

During 1915 Russian Government tested and procured British motorcycles and sidecars for military use: BSA, Rudge, 3½ hp Sunbeam 8 hp Combinations, Royal Enfield model 180 combinations and 3½ hp Premiers were all selected.

British manufacturers such as Royal Enfield also supplied the French, Dutch and Belgian Governments.

1916 Developments

By January 1916 it was clear this War was far from a short skirmish: the Western Front now a 400-mile line of complex defensive trench system running from the Swiss border to the Belgian channel coast and heavy artillery rained down tons of shells on armies locked in a bloody stalemate. The allied forces and their British motorcycles were also fighting in Gallipoli, Mesopotamia, Egypt, Africa and The Balkans. British made motorcycles 'saw' action with the Dutch and Belgians on the Western Front and Russians on the Eastern Front. Meanwhile, preparations were made in Britain for conscription: the local Reserve Committees - which supervised motorcyclist recruitment - became centralised under the control of the Auto Cycle Union (ASU).

The Motorcycling press continued the recruitment drive urging riders to sign up: many came forward to become Despatch Riders or members of the MMGS in advance of conscription, effective from March 1916.

With conscription in place, the Motorcycle Magazine ceased to be an official recruitment channel. The magazine had received 10,605 applications and enquiries from August 1914 - September 1916.[56]

In 1916 the seeds of decline were sown for many motorcycle manufacturers, several being dependent on other small manufactures to supply components. Larger military suppliers such as Enfield and Clyno were using engines sourced from J.A. Prestwich (JAP) and A.J. Stevens respectively. These companies were safe for the time being.

The effects of war hampered access to raw materials, increased fuel prices, and export difficulties and delays. Companies with Government contracts such as Triumph and Douglas were largely unaffected by the strict restrictions regarding export licences. Others without War Office contracts were outspoken in criticism of Government Policy. These were the companies who were quite frankly seeing their customer base disappear below the mud of the Western Front; and as a result many ceased production forever during or shortly after the war.

One example and critic of the Government at this time was the Royal Ruby Cycle Company who had no Government contracts. The small manufacturer had produced a new "ladies model" with step-through frame. This 1916 departure taken by several manufactures was a means of maximising the potential customer base. Ruby turned to the manufacture of munitions after the production of civilian motorcycles was halted, and eventually went bankrupt after the war, following the failure of a Russian Contract due to the Revolution.

Whilst the motorcycle was a key part of the communication and logistics infrastructure it 'trailed behind' aero-developments which had more potential to tip the strategic balance. On the other hand, subsequent advances in motorcycle engineering post war did benefit from the dramatic development of the aeroplane engine during the War

---

[56] The Motor Cycle, 15 February 1917, P140

period: one designer well placed to continue development was Granville Bradshaw.

The ABC Motors Ltd Designer Granville Bradshaw had an insatiable appetite for innovation. Sprung frames were beginning to be talked about, but only Bradshaw had converted the concept into a usable machine. But, these sprung frames were not yet robust enough for the rough conditions being experienced in war zones.

Experimental 2½ hp ABC Lightweight 1916   (The Motorcycle)

The ABC company with one foot in aeroplane and pump manufacturing fitted their lightweight engines designed for Airship generators into motorcycles. Later ABC was able to manufacture a batch of horizontal twin 3hp machines for the Egyptian Government[57]. These machines had a four speed gearbox and featured the leaf sprung frame and forks that became a feature of later ABCs produced during the 1920s.

In November 1916 all civilian motorcycle production finally ceased: with small scale production permitted under special licence, but only for export in small numbers and the odd prototype such as the ABC above.

With civilian production halted, the planned joint Motorcycle and Car Show never came to fruition, but a second-hand car and motor-cycle

Show did take place at The Royal Agricultural Halls, Islington from 10 to 18 November 1916[58]

---
[57] The Motor Cycle, 17 February 1916 P158

When the Government had restricted the import of paper making material. The Motor Cycle magazine - quick to turn this situation into an opportunity - pointed out to its readers they should place regular orders for the magazine at the same newsagent to enable them to avoid wasted returns: They omitted to tell readers all unsold magazines were routinely pulped and reused.

During early 1916 the price of petrol was rising and by March the Royal Automobile Club were calling for economy. The motorcycling press, although understanding, argued that motorcycles used less fuel than other vehicles, and performed a vital and valuable service by carrying munition-workers to their place of work. The magazine went on to berate owners of coaches and lorry manufactures for wasting petrol. However, this call was in vain as restrictions were subsequently put in place by the authorities.

Paraffin as a fuel had been discussed in the motorcycling press since before the war. P&M had produced a concept machine in 1914, but there is no apparent evidence of it being put into production. Home manufactured systems were in place in 1916 and used a small tank of petrol as ignition to start the machine, then once warmed up diverted to run on paraffin. The P&M system included some compression adjustment, whilst others make no mention of any required adjustment.

1917 Developments

Shortage of petrol led to further restrictions and on 24 January 1917, the Petrol Committee announced that no new Spirit licences would be issued. Later in the year oil based substitutes were also placed on the restricted list.

Eager to 'manage' this situation resourceful people were coming up with ever more wild alternatives: even suggesting Acetylene gas, used for motorcycle lights. By July the loopholes had been closed: but this did not stop determined motorcyclists being pictured on a range of

---

[58] The Motor Cycle, 16 November 1916, P437

War Bike: British Military Motorcycling 1899-1919

bizarre coal gas powered motorcycles, complete with large gas bags or pressurised containers.

The combination of a continuing ban on petrol and ACU membership numbers dropping, led to a plea for motorcyclists to join the ACU: lobbying by the Motorcycle Magazine, ACU and others did result in a 50% refund of road fund licences.

Also in January 1917 the Ministry of Munitions decided that in view of their excellent test record, RFC Phelon and Moore motorcycles no longer needed testing at Brooklands Race Track before export.

P&M testers at Brooklands in 1915   (Brooklands Museum)

There was a continuing flow of wounded soldiers from the Battlefield to hospitals in Britain: an established route led to forward dressing stations for the wounded before ambulance transfer to train and back to Britain aboard ship. Upon return, the likely route was transfer from trains to motor Ambulances or motorcycle combinations to local Red Cross Hospitals.

As War progressed, the lack of civilian motorcycles and sporting events to report on caused the Motorcycle Magazine to look elsewhere for content, reporting on occasional events in Australia and other places unaffected by the conflict. They also delved into their archives revisiting pre-war events in an occasional series "Sporting Reminiscences" as well as regular "10 years ago" features. Women too were becoming recognised with references to female motorcyclists doing war work and another article "Through Feminine Goggles" reviewed ladies' models and female motorcycling experience.

During 1917 motorcycle commentators considered the post-war environment, partly fueled by a more optimistic outlook, but undoubtedly driven by the shortage of articles to publish. With optimism came a genuine concern on the part of manufactures for the future of the industry. A few new designs were reviewed, but the big concern was: What would become of the thousands of military motorcycles that returned after the War? No doubt returning troops would be keen for a bargain, but the manufactures were understandably worried that a flood of used motorcycles would kill off the industry. The Association of British and Allied Manufactures put forward a proposal that all surplus military motorcycles should be returned to their original manufacture in batches for overhaul before being sold on to the public.

Patents were still put forward for new developments such as sprung frame and saddles. These designs still fell far short of battlefield requirements. Other innovations were put forward by the man in the street and there is evidence some modifications made by Despatch Riders in the field were finding their way onto the market. One such item on the market in 1917 was the Excel Leg shields.

Excel Leg Shields 1917 (The Motorcycle)

By now letters from the front were describing the dire state of the roads on the western front. Following the winter of 1917 the roads were described as being like "runny porridge".

War Bike: British Military Motorcycling 1899-1919

One officer described the Despatch Riders as heroes *"having to weave in between columns of vehicles and mules."* He went on to say that *"the mud was so deep that fallen horses would drown and railway sleepers set to make tracks passable would float in the liquid mud"*. He went on to describe how Despatch Riders had to find their way with vague directions wading through knee deep mud after leaving the road to deliver messages; after returning to the HQ would find a revised order and have to do it all again.

Photographic equipment was by this time banned by the British, so that many of the surviving pictures of the latter years of the war are censored and posed. Some photographs did get taken at the front by ordinary men risking a great deal by recording the truth: a display of war weary and damaged individuals, devoid of emotion, eyes staring into the middle distance.

Manufacturers continued to have a difficult time; licenses for export to friendly countries were few and far between, but the Russians were continuing to place orders. During 1917 Royal Enfield were supplying 6hp solos and 8 hp combinations for the Russian Army. Norton also delivered military models to Russia. Ariel supplied the Dutch Army with 3½ hp machines whilst Sunbeam supplied their 8hp combination Ambulance to the French Red Cross. ABC continued to provide large numbers of engines for use as pumps and generators to Allied Forces.

Military motorcycles bound for France   (Mortons)

The Brodie "Tin" Helmet first developed in 1915 was first seen in pictures of motorcyclists from September 1917. As protective headwear was in short supply we can presume the Motorcycle Machine Gun Service and those on the front line were supplied well before Despatch Riders.

By autumn 1917 Douglas motorcycles were criticised for a perceived lack of development: this was no doubt compounded by the fact that they were engaged 24 hours-a-day manufacturing and repairing machines as well as supplying stationary engines to the War Office. They were unable to engage in any research and development or publicity. They were also being compared - by some unfavorably - with the Triumph, when in reality they were very different mounts. The Motorcycle magazine defended the lightweight Bristol Twin and went on to print a number of letters from service personnel praising the Duggie.

Cpl W. Pratt Ex- P&M Competition rider on a lightweight Douglas unchanged since 1913 (Mortons)

"Ixion" writing in September brought a subtle reality to the table, by stating that even Triumph would be fighting for survival after the war as all these motorcycles were essentially 1913 models.

1918 Developments

With the American US Forces joining the allies and the introduction of Tanks it was inevitable optimism levels raised to consider cessation of hostilities.

Public announcements of well-known motorcyclists killed in action became a regular event: Lt Frank Houghton architect of the 1915 Brooklands Services Meetings and now member of the new Royal Air

Force (RAF) was killed in a flying accident in May whilst testing aircraft-to-aircraft wireless communication at Biggin Hill in Kent[59].

Lt Frank Magens Caufield Houghton pictured in 1915 (Brooklands Museum)

Later in June it was announced that Vernon Busby, the well known pre-war racer, Despatch Rider and regular Motor Cycle Magazine correspondent, was killed whilst piloting an RAF operational flight near London[60].

The Motorcycle Magazine had always adapted over time to take account of the evolution of motorcycle. Now the War had dramatically reduced its readership. Although many in the forces were still reading the magazine it was now shared rather than subscribed to; production costs increased as paper and fuel were rationed; Advertising revenue dropped as the number of small ads fell; but perhaps the biggest

---

[59] The Times, 28 May 1918.
[60] Flight Magazine, 27 June 1918, P719

problem they faced was the lack of material. The magazine had already scoured the world for sporting events; they had introduced articles about female motorcyclists and reminded readers about the history of motorcycling with articles such as "The Development of the Passenger Motor-Cycle".

Keen to exploit the fact that many motorcyclists were now pilots the publishers looked to the sky to expand the magazine's content. The first departure from motorcycling came in the shape of occasional articles from 1916 about the development of aviation. From October 1917 they extended this subject further into a regular feature called the Facts and Theories of Flight. From April 1918 this developed further into the weekly Aviation Section.

In November came the news that everyone was waiting for. The Great War was over. The De-mobilisation of military machinery was fairly swift and within weeks thousands of surplus military motorcycles returned to Britain.

Kempton Park race course in south west London was turned into a reception point for military vehicles of all types. Motorcycles were arranged in long rows on the grass. Those in good repair were covered with tarpaulins whilst others were left in the open. Sidecars were removed and formed large piles four or five in height.

Military Motorcycles Awaiting Disposal

1919 Developments

Those hoping for bargain ex-military motorcycles were disappointed: seeking to carefully manage a return to normal life, the government arranged for motorcycles to be supplied back to factory suppliers for repair and resale. Some Government surplus motorcycles were auctioned in January 1919. These consisted of 24 Rudge and 86 Zeniths fit for repair and 17 Sunbeams, 96 Scott combinations, 36 Scott solos, 99 Zeniths 23 Premiers and 33 Rovers described as "unfit". These vehicles were not of the current specification and therefore not viable for repair.

Armored Motor machine gun carriers were taken to workshops in Slough where they were decommissioned and prepared for sale by removing the armor leaving the sidecar frame.

Some motorcycles not suitable for refurbishment continued to be sold at auctions around the country and appeared for public sale in local motorcycle suppliers.

One very original 1919 registered model 'H' Triumph - still sporting its wartime specification mudguards and original Brooks tool pouches - was recently unearthed from a shed in West London. The available evidence suggests this is possibly a unique example of a military motorcycle from this period refurbished for re-sale by Triumph.

War Bike: British Military Motorcycling 1899-1919

A Model H Triumph Registered in 1919 discovered in West London in 2015
(Author)

10: The Intelligence Corps

Formal Intelligence gathering and co-ordination had had been in existence during the Boer War. The Secret Service Bureau was formed in 1909 led by Captain Vernon Kell who later became the Head of Military Intelligence Section 5 (MI5) responsible for threats at home; and Commander Mansfield Cumming (Known as "C") was made responsible for a new Secret Intelligence Service (MI6) the main brief being collection of intelligence from overseas[61].

Newly recruited Intelligence Officers on Rudge-Multis August 1914 (Mortons)

The War Office identified suitable candidates who were a mix of Army Officers, Metropolitan Police Officers and some civilians. They were contacted by telegram on 5 August for mobilisation. This embryo Corps included a motorcycle section, riding War Office supplied Black 3½ hp Rudge Multis, with Lucas Generators and lamps as well as Jones Speedometers calibrated in Kilometres. The motorcyclists were tested on their technical knowledge and riding skills: one rider's driving test described as follows:

"The mechanics showed him the control, and he started up the hill as Pullin did when he set forth to win the T.T. Nursemaids, children, dachshunds, and Pekinese fled for safety, and then returning at breakneck speed he skidded

---

[61] History of Army Intelligence, www.army.mod.uk/documents/general/history_of_intelligence_corps.pdf, P1

almost to a standstill, and thanks to the excellent Rudge clutch he just managed to execute an (...figure of) 8".[62]

They together with the rest of the Corps sailed from Southampton aboard the *"Olympia"* on 12 October 1914. Whilst the media were reporting 'motor-cyclist being mobile linguists', in reality their tasks were far more risky. One of these Intelligence Officers was 2nd Lieutenant Roger Rolleston 'Flick' West, a Rudge rider who was awarded the Distinguished Service Order (DSO) for assisting Lieutenant J.A.C. Pennycuick in the demolition of the bridge at Pontoise.

During retreat from Mons, West rode his motor-cycle to retrieve maps left in the French village of Pontoise; on his return he noticed the village bridge over the river Oise was being prepared for demolition to prevent German cavalry crossing and over-running the withdrawing British Expeditionary Force. Despite withdrawal orders from his brigade commander, West assisted an Engineer, Lieutenant Pennycuik, to set explosive charges and 'blow the bridge' within sight of the pursuing Germans.[63]

Another Intelligence Officer, Journalist and author, H.P.C. Pollard, reported in a patriotic letter:

"The roads here are bad but not at all un-rideable, except for shell holes. I am having a very sound time, and have met lots of men I sent out ...none of them bear any grudge."[64]

The work of the Intelligence Corps led to a discovery that the Germans had the capability to monitor the Allies telegraph traffic: a fact that cemented the continuing importance of Despatch Riders for the communication of important and sensitive messages.

---

[62] The Motor Cycle, 24 September 1914, P360
[63] The London Gazette, 9 December 1914, P10548. West's Own account is included in Diary of the War: Retreat from Mons to the Battle of Aisne, Imperial War Museum (London), Ref 67/122/1,
[64] The Motor Cycle, 31 December 1914, P731

11: Competitions & Record Breaking

Many history books state Brooklands Race Track, the premier location for racing and record breaking, was closed until 1919 after being taken over by the RFC. Although it is true the Motor Course and Aerodrome was closed to the public from 30 September 1914, the track continued to be a venue for record breaking and testing.

J. Bailey was still pushing the 350cc sidecar records to just over 50 mph in September 1914. In 1915 each of the "Brooklands Special" engines manufactured by Norton were tested and certified at the track[65]. D.R. O'Donovan was also testing a new chain driven Norton motorcycle at the circuit during the summer of 1915.

Chain Driven Norton being tested at Brooklands 1915   (Brooklands Museum)

---

[65] Cohen G, Flat Tank Norton, P7

War Bike: British Military Motorcycling 1899-1919

A Morgan testing the potholes track in 1915   (Brooklands Museum)

The track continued to be used for the testing of all RFC Motorcycles delivered from P&M, but RFC Lorries and other vehicle movements were further harming an already-damaged race track.

In June 1915, Lieut F Houghton[66] of the 25th Divisional Cycle Company suggested an "All Khaki" meeting be held for servicemen based close to the Brooklands track.

Well aware of the potential damage he stated long distance races would not be possible.

2nd Lieut F Houghton

---

[66] Later the Author of "Tales of a True Despatch Rider" The Motor Cycle, 13 April 1916, P354

The editor of the Motorcycle Magazine promoted the idea, then taken up by The Secretary of the Auto Cycle Union and BARC. This meeting was approved and featured 172 entrants for sprints, hill climbs and novelty gymkhana events such as the Serpentine race in which riders had to negotiate the tuning sheds as slow as possible without placing a foot down.

Asst Paymaster C.P. Marcel RNR on his Indian, taking part in the Serpentine Race
(Brooklands Museum)

At 2pm on 7 August crowds, including injured servicemen from the nearby hospital, gathered in the sunshine to watch the first events to take place at Brooklands for over a year.

The lack of marshals proved a challenge as there were no spectator barriers, however, six sergeants of Lieut. Houghton's 25th Divisional Cyclist Company managed to keep order and we are told *"they were obeyed with alacrity"*. The half-mile sprint under the auspices of the British Motor Cycle Racing Club was run on the Railway Straight.

War Bike: British Military Motorcycling 1899-1919

Riders taking part in the Spark Plug Change race on the Railway straight
(Brooklands Museum)

Cpl Barker on his 8hp Zenith in the Unlimited Hill Climb Event

(Brooklands Museum)

After the success of the event a similar "All Services" meeting was held on 4 September 1915.

This time sprints were held on the finishing straight, meaning that spectators could be housed in the two grandstands. Riders were sent clockwise under the Members Bridge via the fork after completing the race and despite plans to repair the finishing straight, it remained in a bad state of repair for race day, requiring fencing-off causing a track so narrow some races had to be run in two or three heats.

Sgt A. Milner on his 349cc Diamond, Winner of the lightweight mile sprint with Pte F. Edwards on a Douglas No 55　　　　　　　　　　　　　　(Brooklands Museum)

On that sun baked Saturday in September 1915 how distant the War must have seemed as once more Surrey air was filled with noise and fumes of competition.

At 6pm spectators including wounded servicemen from the local hospital gathered to see the competitors receive their prizes. Winners once again found themselves featured in press adverts proclaiming the virtues of Sunbeam, Zenith and Norton Motorcycles.

This was not quite the end of Brooklands Motorcycle Meetings; keen not to be left out the workers of The Brooklands Royal Aircraft Factory held their own race meeting on 23 October 1915. This was essentially a scratch event conceived after the success of the earlier Services Events.

Members of the Royal Aircraft Factory lining up for a sprint (Brooklands Museum)

Very little is known of this event, but from press reports we know there were 265 entries competing in 12 events including the two Gymkhana events. The sprints were again held on the finishing straight which was reported to be in much better condition.

With arrangements in place for track repair, these events immediately raised expectations among servicemen, and more "Services" Meetings were soon being planned for 1916. The RFC were repairing the track which was in much better condition. However, the growing pressure on resources, particularly petrol and difficulty in justifying (mainly) officers having fun and risking injury meant that this was the last of the official military events for the duration of the War.

Other events such as an Army vs. Navy Hill Climb organised by the Streatham motorcycle club held at Newlands Corner, near Guildford in Surrey took place in September 1915. Some other scratch, unsanctioned events such as Hill Climbs and Trials were also mentioned in contemporary press reports.

12: Sidecars, Gun Carriers & Ambulances

Sidecars

Sidecar combinations had been around since the pioneer days of motorcycling. Trailers gave way to wicker side or forward mounted chairs; and by mid 1914 developed into the traditional boat shaped body on a tubular steel chassis. They were widely in use on public roads as well as competing in organised events, record-breaking and trials. Sidecars were first used for the transport of officers during maneovures. These were initially privately owned, but later widely used by the RFC, Army and other allied forces.

In 1908 Arthur Westerdick, keen motorcyclist and furniture maker in his Father's Company developed his first sidecar Body. Undeterred by his father's disapproval he set up a new workshop and was soon supplying large numbers of sidecar bodies to Phelon & Moore.

RFC Rider on P&M with Military sidecar (Manx Aviation & Military Museum)

On 20 April 1915 Westerdick supplied Military Body No1 to Phelon & Moore at the price of £4 10 Shillings, by 30 December of that year he had supplied 272 Military sidecar Bodies, most of which were supplied to the RFC.[67]

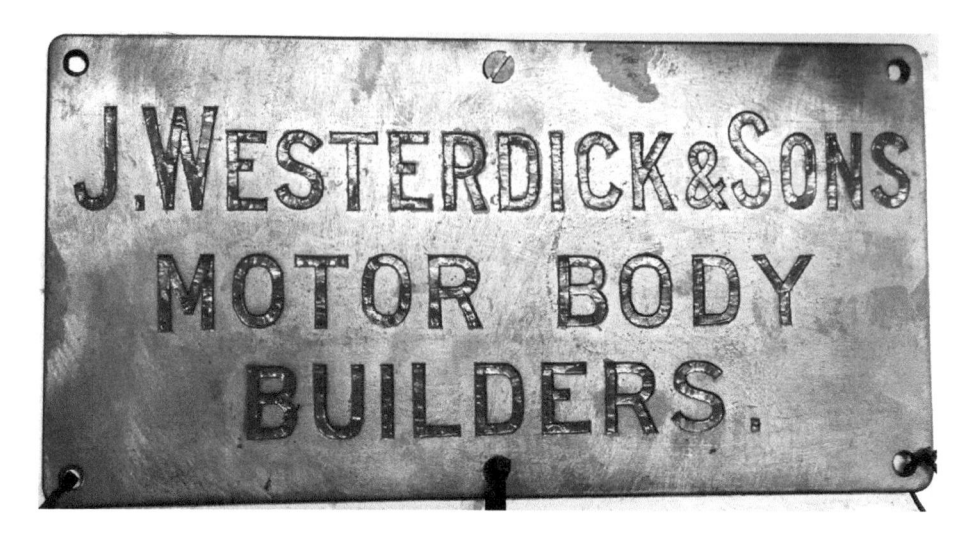

The Brass Plate from the Westerdick & Sons workshop   (John Watson)

Little is known about War Office procurement of sidecars, but Triumph Gloria sidecars were supplied in large numbers for the use of officers whilst other manufacturers including Sunbeam provide combinations for allied forces,

Gun Carriers

In 1914 some manufacturers began developing Motorcycle gun carriers. It is unclear whether this was the result of a request from the War Office or innovation on the part of the Trade.

In May 1914 Royal Enfield produced a prototype 6hp machine with a strengthened sidecar chassis on which was mounted a rear facing Maxim gun. The gun was reputed to be the same one used in their

---

[67] Westerdick Company Ledgers, Private Collection

earlier "Made like a gun" advertising campaign[68]. This vehicle was provided to the Ministry of Munitions for evaluation together with similar prototypes by Scott, Zenith, Premier[69] and Matchless[70].

Soon after War began the War Office realised the strategic significance of mobile machine guns and on 12 November a Mobile Machine Gun Battery was approved for each division of the Army. These batteries known initially as The Motor Machine Gun Service (MMGS), were designated as units of the Royal Field Artillery and consisted of 18 Motorcycle Sidecar combinations carrying Six Vickers Machine Guns, Ammunition spares and equipment. The unit also included eight solo motorcyclists acting as scouts and Despatch Riders, two or three wagons or cars and a motorcycle sidecar combination for the Officer in Charge.

Scott Machinegun Carrier featured in a Series of Wills Cigarette Cards

(Private Collection)

In addition to standard service pay riders and gunners were paid an additional 2d. per day, plus a further 6d. per day after passing a gun test.

In a parallel development the Royal Naval Air Service formed an Armoured Car Service including Scott motorcycle gun carriers, as well as heavily armoured saloon cars.

---

[68] Vandervelde J, Royal Enfield War Dept Models Report, 11 October 2012, (Un-published)
[69] Reports of Zenith & Premier Combinations, The Motor-Cycle, 24 December 1914, P703 & P707
[70] Reports of Matchless Combination, The Motor-Cycle, 31 December 1914, P721

War Bike: British Military Motorcycling 1899-1919

The Motor Cycle Magazine once more publicly supported recruitment: promoting the new MMGS, even receiving a letter of thanks from General Kitchener. The Kitchener letter also urged further recruits to come forward and volunteer, stating:

"I shall be glad to hear of any reasons that may be given you by young and suitable men for not availing themselves of this opportunity to see service in the Field, where they are so much wanted."

The magazine continued to print a recruitment page with names of new recruits almost every week throughout 1915. The 6 hp Royal Enfield with a JAP engine and chain drive and the Scott 532cc water cooled 2-stroke engine with chain drive were selected by the War Office for the MMGS and a Vickers Machine Gun mounted on a modified sidecar frame: the Scott carried more armour around and below the gun, although the Enfield gun was easier to dismount or face in a rear position, it provided less protection for the rider; it was envisaged guns could be fired on the move but no evidence exists this method was ever used in the Field.

Scott Machine Gun Carrier, Illustrated War News 2 Dec 1914   (Private Collection)

18 x Scotts of No.1 Battery were the first of the new units to the Front after training at Bisley Camp; one example, which demonstrates the strategic use of the MMGS was at Hill 60 in April 1915: Enemy guns were persistently firing on British troops from a hill formed of spoil from a nearby railway cutting - known by locals as Lovers Knoll. For three months the 171 Tunnelling Company of the Royal Engineers had been digging into the hill, and their efforts rewarded when at 7.05pm on 17 April it blew with the loss of 150 Prussian Guards and 2 Royal Engineers. This was not the apocalyptic blast, which in June 1917 removed the hill completely and created what was widely regarded as the largest manmade crater.

Next morning, the MMGS Gun mounted Scott combinations of No 4 Battery repositioned to rear of enemy lines: de-mounting their guns, they overran the trenches, providing covering fire for the assault by West Kents, East Surreys, and Queen Victoria's Rifles.

Reported as the first time No 4 Battery were in action.

Sergeant J.S. Clarke and Gunner J. Rafferty were awarded Distinguished Service Medals.

Their Citations read:

J.S. Clarke: For conspicuous devotion to duty during the attack on "Hill 60" on 17th and 18th April, 1915, especially in assisting to dig out guns and men who had been buried by shell fire.[71]

Gunner J. Rafferty: For conspicuous devotion to duty during the attack on "Hill 60" on 17th and 18th April 1915. He continued working his gun under heavy shell fire until he was severely wounded.[72]

---

[71] London Gazette, 30 June 1915. Medal Card, National Archives: Ref WO372/23/50985
[72] London Gazette, 30 June 1915. Medal Card, National Archives: Ref WO372/23/65009

War Bike: British Military Motorcycling 1899-1919

Sgt Mackey & Gunner Rafferty pictured on the occasion of receiving their medals

(The Motorcycle)

Another member of the MMGS honoured at this time was Sgt MacKey pictured above with Rafferty in 1916. His Citation read:

Sgt E.R. Mackey: For conspicuous gallantry. After his section officer had been killed he showed great ability and bravery in leading his section, and inspiring the men with his example under trying circumstances.[73]

The Royal Enfields of No 5 Battery were also in action at Hill 60 later in the day, following a counter-attack; they also de-mounted their gun and provided covering fire.

Scott and Royal Enfield gun carriers were soon replaced by the more robust Clyno: a highly versatile gun platform based on the 1914 model, with a twin cylinder Stevens (AJS) 744 c.c. engine unit with quickly detachable, interchangeable wheels and a spare carried on the motorcycle offside. On the platform: the gunner, a Vickers machine

---
[73] London Gazette, 10 March 1916.

gun, ammunition oil and water. As in the case of Scotts and Royal Enfield, variants included: sidecars without guns - to be used in case of damage - and a combination designed to only carry ammunition.

From February 1915 this vehicle was adopted as the standard machine of the MMGS. By 1915, each weekend Clynos were delivered to Kempton Park Race Course in convoys of 20 to 25 before being shipped to France.

At the Western Front, in November 1914 the War was a mobile conflict with rapid movement back and forth along the shifting Front. Although the batteries were being used as a "flying Squad" to deliver force where required quickly, this may not have represented the *'drive, point and shoot'* mobile gun carriage envisaged at the MMGS's inception.

In fact many machine gun batteries on the Western Front spent most of their time attached to Battalion Machine Gun Batteries situated in the trenches, until 1918 advances brought them back into the Field. Elsewhere such as Egypt, Palestine, East Africa and Mesopotamia, they continued throughout the War as mobile units.

Meanwhile, other manufacturers continued developing motorcycle gun carriers: Scott - who had lost out - developed an odd looking three-wheeled gun-carrying cycle car which the Military rejected, and even after further development as a civilian vehicle "The Sociable" failed to make an impact.

Scott Motor Machinegun Carrier IWM (Q 70506)

Theodore Henry Tessier, of the BAT Motor Manufacturing Company, lodged a design for a rotating – *'equatorial'* - gun mount for use on aircraft, vehicles and motorcycle sidecars. In the case of the sidecar, the gun could be fired on the move and enabled the gunner to rotate with the gun providing a large arc of fire. However, this design was not subsequently used for motorcycles.

A variation of the gun carrying motorcycle was a gun carriage patented in 1916 by W. Rankin and R. Player, of Wrights Forge and Engineering Co., Ltd., Tipton, Staffordshire. It was a gun mounted on a two wheeled platform that appeared quickly detachable and usable on a variety of motorcycles.

Its standard configuration is reminiscent of the 1899 trailer, but this version - with a wheel removed - could also be attached as a sidecar. A prototype was tested with a passenger on a 6 hp Enfield, but this too failed to make it to production.

Matchless manufactured a Vickers based gun platform similar in design to the Clyno. As well as interchangeable wheels the sidecar featured an extendable mount which enabled the gun to be mounted and used for anti-aircraft fire. The Model 8B/2M motorcycle is based on a model 8B, upgraded according to the Russian Army specification, to an 8 hp JAP engine with a three speed countershaft gearbox[74].

Matchless 8B/2M Machinegun Carriage   **(Bonhams)**

---

[74] The British Motorcycle Charitable Trust Newsletter, August 2015, P2

War Bike: British Military Motorcycling 1899-1919

Ambulances

Lady Amy Rowley Vice President of the Guildford and Woking Branch of the Red Cross is credited as the originator of the Motorcycle Ambulance. A concept first seen at the Brooklands Red Cross Field day in June 1914 was a stretcher on a Triumph Gloria Sidecar chassis attached to a 3½ hp Triumph motorcycle.

Soon after the outbreak of war manufacturers were demonstrating motorcycle ambulances and converting on an ad hoc basis for use at home by volunteers. Royal Enfield, Rudge, Sunbeam, Triumph, and Zenith developed motorcycles adapted for use as a stretcher carrier. Other manufactures such as H.J. Dalton and Mead & Deakin produced generic stretcher carriers.

Lady Rowley Pictured at the Brooklands Red Cross Day 1914

In late 1914 The Red Cross Society selected the Newcastle upon-Tyne Motor Company (N.U.T) Motorcycle Stretcher carrier as their standard model. This was an 8hp N.U.T motorcycle attached to a double-decked sidecar chassis which could be covered to provide some protection to the casualties.

In 1916 The Watsonion Sidecar Company produced an Ambulance sidecar in partnership with Norton which was rejected by the Red Cross because of insufficient springing, but was adopted by French and Italian authorities[75]. The somewhat claustrophobic looking unit powered by a 4 hp Norton was a stretcher mounted on a grey plywood box with a hinged arched lid that remained open during the carriage of a casualty.

In 1917 variations included development of a sidecar attached to an 8 hp Matchless machine by the Empire Sidecar Company, which could take a patient seated or lying down, and was developed further by the Campion Cycle Company: this combination was powered by an 8 hp Campion motorcycle, with a robust enclosed sidecar and removable windscreen & rear door for easy-access to the stretcher.

Sidecar ambulances were used widely across Europe and at home by the Red Cross and Allied Armies. Motorcycle combinations were often used to transport casualties to switching venues for onward transfer by cars and lorries.

Some were the subject of gearbox issues, which considering the transport load: casualty, rider and often passenger to care for the patient, was not surprising in the challenging rough, muddy conditions.

Another variant was the wireless carrier. In these early days of radio the unit was more likely to be non-mobile and auxiliary-powered from a motorcycle engine driven generator. Sidecars were used as mobile transport. It is not known how widely used during the War period as enemy forces were able to monitor radio traffic.

---

[75] The Motorcycle, 16 March 1916

War Bike: British Military Motorcycling 1899-1919

Douglas Combinations for wireless equipment

Phelon & Moore Motorcycles awaiting delivery

13: Women Motorcyclists at War

In 1913 the Suffragette Movement was still growing when Emily Davidson threw herself in front of the Kings horse at the Epsom Derby. However, the Movement suspended direct action at the outbreak of hostilities, although the more radical Women's Suffrage Federation did continue with their protests[76].

Paradoxically the War propelled women to the forefront of society, in a way that could not have been predicted. In the early days of the War women served in nursing roles, but as men went off to fight women worked on the land, in factories and heavy industry. Less well known is the vital role by women as riders and drivers: transporting officers, wounded and acting as motorcycle Despatch Riders.

Voluntary Aid Detachment Nurses   (British Red Cross Museum & Archives)

A number of courageous women were based overseas and some close to the Front lines and their stories reflect bravery and determination only recently recognised.

---

[76] Leventhal FM (2002), "Twentieth-century Britain: an encyclopaedia" P432

Women were keen to fill roles that may have been unacceptable a few years earlier: volunteering to become Despatch Riders for organisations, such as the Women's Emergency Corps and Women's Volunteer Reserve Corps. They drove sidecars for Police Forces, The Red Cross Voluntary Aid Detachment and RFC.

On the Home Front: Anna Blakiston writing in 1916 explained as Army Service Corps Supervisor, she drove a motorcycle to travel to farms and railway stations in Yorkshire. Anna was responsible for overseeing loading of forage hay[77].

Work being carried out on a P&M Motorcycle   (IWM Q72647)

By 1917 the call for Despatch Riders went out and RFC women Despatch Riders were evident in central London[78]. The RFC (Later RAF) employed on mainland Europe. Anna Blakiston's story is one of many in the Motorcycle Magazine disclosing how women served their country in wartime. Photos taken on behalf of the War Office/RFC disclose P&M motorcycles with female riders and mechanics.

---

[77] Blakiston A, Women's work in the Army Service Corps, The Motor-Cycle, 29 June 1916, P599
[78] The Motor-Cycle, 24 May 1917, P472

Notably, two women motorcyclists became Wartime celebrities: Mari Chisholm and Elsie Knocker are renowned and famed for their courage and lack of concern from their service on the Front Line. Speaking in June 1976[79] Mari explained how she rode up to London on her racing motorcycle to sign up for the Women's Emergency Corps as a Despatch Rider - much to the disapproval of her mother.

Elsie and Mari pictured after receiving the Chevaliers de l'Ordre de Léopold II

She and her competition rider friend Elsie Knocker became Despatch Riders in London and were subsequently signed up by Dr Munro for his "Flying Ambulance Corps" supporting the Belgian Red Cross. Once 'in the Field' they established their own field dressing station, within a hundred yards of the trenches at Pervyse north of Ypres.

The deprivation, bloody hostility and barren conditions of this wartime environment were ignored by Mari and Elsie: Mari describes hiding behind a wall, witnessing a bayonet charge, hearing the clash of steel and treating and clearing the wounded having received terrible wounds from German-serrated ended bayonet; dashing out on foot into "*no-*

---

[79] Oral History Interview, Imperial War Museum Catalogue No: 771

War Bike: British Military Motorcycling 1899-1919

mans-land" to rescue pilots from their crashed planes: the selfless compassion, and bravery of Mari & Elsie exemplify how women served in so many ways through the wartime era.

Mari and Elsie received decoration from the Belgians: their service finally commemorated on 22 November 2014 by a memorial unveiled in Pervyse thanks to author Diane Atkinson, who played a pivotal role in revealing the detail of these two wartime heroines, Mari Chisholm and Elsie Knocker.[80]

Elsie Knocker with her 2¾ hp open frame Douglas used in Belgium[81]   (Mortons)

---

[80] Atkinson Dr D, Elsie and Mairi Go To War: Two Extraordinary Women on the Western Front, Random House, 2009

[81] The Motorcycle, 5 October 1916, P300

14: Pigeon Carriers

The role of *'the feathered Brigade'* during WW1 is well known: pigeons were widely used throughout the war and even into WW2. The changing battle lines in the early stages of War made pigeons ideal for sending messages back to Headquarters.

The logistics of this type of communication involved central pigeon lofts - often constructed from converted buses or lorries - from which batches of pigeons in baskets could be transported closer to the Front by motorcycle riders.

Mobile loft and motorcyclists transporting Pigeons

Contemporary film and photographs show apparently motorcyclists carrying large picnic hampers on their backs. These were in fact large wicker baskets carrying pigeons to their destination.

War Bike: British Military Motorcycling 1899-1919

A message sent from Forward Position would quickly be received at the loft, and then sent on by telegraph or Despatch Rider to Headquarters.

Despatch Rider W.L. Kewley with Pigeon Basket (Manx Aviation & Military Museum)

15: Recycling and Repair

The First World War was in many ways a 'green' war: after the organised chaos at the beginning, recycling was now taking place on an industrial scale; everything from tin cans, bullet cartridges and barbed wire were reused in some form. Motorcycles were either patched up or sent to repair shops based in the Field or back to England. This was a harsh, challenging environment for a motorcycle design that remained largely the same since 1913. The riders could carry out running repairs but more serious failures such as frame breakage meant a replacement.

Sheds and converted barns served as ad-hoc repair shops: artificers would ply their trade carrying out running repairs and replacing tyres and other much larger Repair Shops were set up to undertake major work; and were also responsible for repurposing motorcycles from any recovered parts.

A Field Repair shop (Mortons)

War Bike: British Military Motorcycling 1899-1919

Initially these repair shops were dealing with numerous makes and models pressed into service by their owners; however, repairing became relatively easier as military motorcycles became standardised. From 1915 the majority of solo motorcycles were Triumph and Douglas, with Phelon & Moore being used by the RFC/RAF.

Repair shops would cover any small repair to other mechanical equipment, and there are also examples of cannibalised motorcycles being converted for use as generators, pumps and even running grinding wheels.

THE ADAPTABLE MOTOR CYCLE.
A Scott, minus front wheel and handle-bars, rigged up in an R.N.A.S. repair shop to drive a lathe. Another is used to drive a dynamo.

A Scott motorcycle used to drive a lathe

Workshops 'called upon' skilled men more than likely previously in the employ of pre-War manufacturers or agents. Note was taken by representatives, of the conditions of use, as well as the modifications made by riders and artificers to cope with the difficult terrain. For example, Triumph introduced larger mudguards and semi-TT handle bars favoured by many riders to maintain better control at speed.

One ASC repair shop in south east London had capacity to 'turn out' 60 re-manufactured machines a week, and included every process from engine rebuilds to stove enamelling of frames and mudguards.

Once ready for delivery, the motorcycles were ridden up Dog Kennel Hill. The testers wore yellow armbands bearing the letter 'T' in Black to identify them on their Army uniforms. This particular repair shop included recruits from motorcycle dealerships as well as Staff Sergeant Jepson, formally of Zenith and J. Oliphant, a Premier works rider who had won a gold medal in the 1914 ACU six day Trial. Oliphant had spent the winter of 1914/15 in Russia preparing a shipment of 150 British motorcycles supplied to the Russian Government[82].

Even as late as 1917 older non-standard machines e.g. Zeniths were still being rebuilt, but designated 'Home Service' only, leaving repair shops in the Field to concentrate on Triumph, Douglas and P&M. Scott motor machine-gun combinations were being completely stripped and rebuilt as combinations for transporting goods[83].

Douglas in Repair Shop Exhibit at the Royal Logistics Corps Museum

(Author)

---

[82] Oliphant J, Letter to the Motor Cycle Magazine, December 1914
[83] The Motor Cycle, 23 August 1917, P180

War Bike: British Military Motorcycling 1899-1919

Women Manufacturing Wheels at the Phelon & Moore Factory in Yorkshire

16: Motorcycle Numbers & Manufacturers

The numbers of WW1 motorcycles are quoted from various sources; however, to quantify with any accuracy the numbers of motorcycles is difficult after this time, because of the double counting of re-conditioned machines, lost records and difficulties cross-referencing those records still in existence.

Michael Carragher in his book 'San Fairy Ann?' explores the numbers in some detail but even he says, *"It is impossible to say how many motorcycles were used throughout the War."*[84]

The most commonly quoted numbers of military motorcycles derives from an audit carried out as at 11 November 1918[85]. The audit however excluded RAF machines, but gave a flavour of the variety of machines in use. The records quote 34,865 motorcycles being available in all theatres including 15,308 in Britain[86].

There are no known records of British military motorcycles in use by other countries.

Numbers of primary suppliers are quoted below as at November 1918[87]:

Douglas (18,315)

Bristol blacksmith brothers, William and Edward Douglas launched their first 350cc flat twin motorcycle in 1907 as a result of purchasing Light Motors Ltd. Douglas is reputed to be the second largest supplier to the military supplying an estimated 25,000 machines.

Their primary model was a fore-&-aft mounted twin cylinder 350cc 2¾ hp side valve with a 2 speed gearbox. These engines were also used as portable generators for wireless sets.

---

[84] Carragher M, San Fairy Ann? Motorcycles & British Victory, Firestep, 2013, P85
[85] Statistics of the Military Effort of the British Empire, British Library, Ref: 9085.h.13
[86] Statistics of the Military Effort of the British Empire, Ibid, P877
[87] Vanderveen BH, Mororcycles to 1945, P26

War Bike: British Military Motorcycling 1899-1919

A Douglas in the Field showing large spares box fitted to all WD machines

(Private Collection)

In 1915 Douglas manufactured a 4hp combination with three speed gearbox. The machine was tested at Brooklands where it failed to reach the top of the Test Hill. A new cylinder was swiftly designed and cast under the supervision of John Douglas, then rushed back to the Surrey racetrack where it then completed its successful test. These combinations went on to be supplied to the War Office for personnel and to transport wireless sets.

Experimentation involving the 2¾ hp machine took place to deliver an anti-gas spray which appeared unsuccessful.

A sprung framed model was sent to France to be tested in battle conditions. However no sprung framed Douglas was manufactured until 1919.

Triumph (17,998)

Founded by German immigrants Siegfried Bettmann and Mauritz Johann Schulte, Triumph began manufacturing bicycles before moving to production of their first Motorcycle in 1902. Like Douglas they were considered to be a long established company with the facilities to produce large numbers.

It is suggested Triumph supplied over 30,000 machines, the majority being the Model H produced from December 1915: a single cylinder 550cc 4 hp machine with a 3 speed Sturmey-Archer countershaft gearbox. This versatile machine could was used as a solo or with a sidecar.

Despatch Rider Arthur C Beard with Triumph (Manx Aviation & Military Museum)

War Bike: British Military Motorcycling 1899-1919

Phelon & Moore (3,383)

Founded in 1904 the distinctive forward angled cylinder headed engine was patented in 1900 by Joah Carver Phelon and nephew Harry Rayner.

The colonial model was a 3½hp motorcycle and is described in the 1915 catalogue as:

"...olive green and black finish with the absolute minimum of plated parts. Extra large tank 2½ in tyres, 10 ½ in footrest clearance. Specially strengthened fork and saddle springs."

Frank Jarvis RFC Dispatch Rider on a Phelon & Moore

(Private Collection D. Waller)

P&M supplied exclusively to the Royal Flying Corps (RAF from 1 April 1918) with a single cylinder 475cc 3½ hp side valve with a 2 speed gearbox. This was the only military motorcycle supplied at the outbreak of War with final chain drive.

The Russians placed an order for 200 3½ hp machines: only half were delivered in deference to continuing RFC orders. P&M also supplied large numbers of combinations to the RFC.

BSA (1,088)

BSA manufactured huge numbers of bicycles, but a relatively small number of motorcycles. They were used in action in East Africa as well as on the Home Front.

Clyno (1,792)

The gun carrier was based on the 1914 model, with twin cylinder AJS 744cc engine and 3-speed gearbox: as a collaboration with gun manufacturers Vickers it featured an innovative system of interchangeable wheels together with a spare mounted on the offside of the cycle; variations included an ammunition carrier, and both types were supplied to British and Russian Governments; initially the front fork was a side-spring Druid, but this was soon superseded by the Brampton Bi-flex providing dual directional springing.

Clyno Machinegun Carrier at the National Motorcycle Museum   (Author)

Scott (411)

Together with Royal Enfield, Scott provided the first Motor Machine Gun Service carriers. Their version was a twin cylinder water-cooled 532cc 2 stroke with a 2 speed transmission which saw action in the more extreme climate of Gallipoli and Mesopotamia.

Rudge Whitworth (395)

The Rudge Multi may have only been supplied to make up numbers in 1914. It was a single cylinder 499cc 3½hp with the patented multi speed gearbox.

1913 Rudge Multi at the National Motorcycle Museum
(Author)

Royal Enfield (161)

Royal Enfield only supplied a limited number of machines to the War Office but they also supplied the Dutch Army and large quantities to the Russian Army.

These included:

- *6hp machine gun carrier (British, Dutch, & South African Defence Force)*
- *6hp combination stretcher carrier (British)*
- *3hp model 140 solo (Dutch Belgian & Russians)*
- *6hp Colonial Model 180 solos (Russians)*

The Motor Machine Gun Service Enfield was a twin cylinder 770cc JAP powered machine with 2 speed gear box with final chain-drive and a machine gun mounted on the combination frame.

Other British Manufactures

Ariel, Sunbeam and Matchless all supplied allied forces abroad and many more manufacturers were represented in the 1918 audit, primarily due to so many privately-owned machines still being in use and then re-issued throughout the conflict. More research is needed to confirm whether any of these manufacturers were direct War Office suppliers.

ABC Motors Ltd

ABC Motors mainly kept to the manufacture of aircraft engines, but their motorcycle engines were used as the basis for pumps in the trenches and for running dynamos.

Norton

Norton made a military model which was supplied to the Russian Government, known as the Empire Model.

Premier

A small number of Premiers were reported as being supplied to the War Office in August 1914; and 312 were supplied to the Russian Government.

War Bike: British Military Motorcycling 1899-1919

German use of British Motorcycles

Whilst the core logistics of the British Army provided everything from machine spares to grain for bread; the German policy was requirement-driven and their Army was expected to gather supplies as it passed through occupied countries.

This explains reports of captured British motorcycles being used and unconfirmed stories of Interned British workers manufacturing British motorcycles in Germany.

Riders with Douglas machines landing at Gallipoli
(The War Illustrated 11 Sept 1915. Page 77)

17: Postscript

The research for this book has concentrated on British motorcycles; however it should be acknowledged that many other Manufactures contributed in great measure to their respective war effort. For example America's Harley Davidson and Indian motorcycles were in action with Canadian troops from the outset.

As a project this book started off as a research exercise in the military role of motorcycles, as compared with other works that concentrated on the role and supply of civilian machines.

As it progressed the 'spotlight' shone on the people as well as the machines: and each & every individual story and experience is unique within the sheer numbers involved. The author can only briefly reference the unimaginable conditions and sights the men and women caught up in WW1 endured; and 'salute' the quiet courage & bravery of all those involved.

In 1918 a Royal message was dispatched urging those planning the ceremony at the end of the war to embrace & acknowledge all those who would never see their loved ones again…

We Will Remember Them

~~ ooo000ooo ~~

Bibliography

Atkinson Dr D, Elsie and Mairi Go To War: Two Extraordinary Women on the Western Front, Random House, 2009

Bradford A, Royal Enfield: The Story of the Company and its People who made it Great, Brewin Books, 2015

Bridger G, The Great War Handbook, Pen and Sword Books Ltd, 2013

Carragher M, San Fairy Ann? Motorcycles and British Victory, Firestep, 2013

Caunter C, Motorcycles: History and Development Part 1, HMSO, 1972

Caunter C, Motorcycles: A Technical History.

Champ R, The Sunbeam Motorcycle, G T Foulis & Co Ltd, 1980

Clayton A, Forearmed: A History of the Intelligence Corps,

Clew J, The Douglas Motorcycle: The Best Twin, Foulis, 1974

Clew J, JAP: The Vintage Years, Haynes Foulis, 1986

Hartley P, The Story of Royal Enfield Motorcycles: Made Like a Gun, Patrick Stephens Ltd, 1981

Hartley P, Bikes At Brooklands, In the Pioneer Days, Goose, 1974

Jones BM, The Story of Panther Motorcycles, Panther Publishing, 2009

Jones BM, Granville Bradshaw: A Flawed Genius? Panther Publishing, 2012

McDiarmid M, Triumph The Legend, Parragon Plus, 1997

Olyslager P, & Vanterbeen B, Motorcycles to 1945

Pulford JSL, The Locke-Kings of Weybridge, Walton & Weybridge History Society, 1996

Venner D, Despatch Rider on the Western Front 1915-18: The Diary of Sergeant Albert Simkin MM, 2015, Pen & Sword, 2015

Watson WL, Adventures of a Despatch Rider

Winton G, Theirs Not to Reason Why: Horsing the British Army 1875 to 1925, Helion and Company, 2013

Glossary

ASC	Army Service Corps
ACU	Auto Cycle Union
BEF	British Expeditionary Force
DSO	Distinguished Service Order
DSM	Distinguished Service Medal
hp	Horse Power
IWM	Imperial War Museum
MMGS	Motor Machine Gun Service
MTC	Mechanical Transport Committee
P&M	Phelon & Moore Motorcycles
OHMS	On His Majesty's Service
RA	Royal Artillery
RAF	Royal Air Force (RFC & RNAS From April 1918)
RE	Royal Engineers
RFC	Royal Flying Corps
RNAS	Royal Naval Air Service
SMS	Short Message Service (Mobile Phone Text Messaging)
TT	Tourist Trophy (Races Isle of Man)
VAD	Voluntary Aid Detachment (of The Red Cross)
WD	War Department
WO	War Office

BROOKLANDS MUSEUM

www.brooklandsmuseum.com

Brooklands Museum Trust Ltd
Brooklands Road
Weybridge
Surrey
KT13 0QN

NATIONAL MOTORCYCLE MUSEUM
WHERE LEGENDS LIVE ON

www.nationalmotorcyclemuseum.co.uk

Coventry Road
Bickenhill
Solihul
West Midlands
BE92 0EJ

The Manx Aviation and Military Museum
www.maps.org.im

The Manx Aviation and Military Museum is located about half a mile to the south of Ronaldsway Airport terminal on the main road to Castletown on the Isle of Man.

The museum is open daily from 10.00am to 4.30pm during the summer, (from late May until the end of September) and every Saturday and Sunday throughout the rest of the year. It also open on Good Friday and Easter Monday.

Fenland Classic Motorcycles
Home of the War-bike Project

CASH IN YOUR ATTIC?
We pay cash for Vintage Motorcycle related Memorabilia, Books, Parts or Pre-1950s Motorcycles.
Get in contact now to find out how much your collection could be worth.

Contact: Info@fenlandclassics.co.uk
Website: www.Fenlandclassics.com

War Bike: British Military Motorcycling 1899-1919